OUTDOOR
SURVIVAL
SKILLS
SIXTH EDITION

Larry Dean Olsen.

A Special Note from the Author

Interest in primitive skills has generated a sizable group of people who want to sit around the campfire with each other. Opportunities to gather are organized regularly in various parts of the world. Those who want to make contact with me or participate in wilderness expeditions, gatherings, and research may reach me by fax, E-mail, or letter.

Sincerely,

Larry D. Olsen
P.O. Box 171
Buhl, ID 83316
Fax: 208-543-6091
E-mail: ldo@anasazi.org
Web site: www.anasazi.org/ldo

OUTDOOR SURVIVAL SKILLS

SIXTH EDITION

LARRY DEAN OLSEN

CHICAGO
REVIEW
PRESS

Library of Congress Cataloging-in-Publication Data

Olsen, Larry Dean, 1939–
    Outdoor survival skills / by Larry Dean Olsen.—6th ed.
      p.   cm.
    Includes index.
    ISBN 1-55652-323-8 (pbk.: alk. paper)
    1. Wilderness survival. I. Title
  GV200.5.047 1998
  613.6'9—dc21   97-20442
                                                                 CIP

Published by Chicago Review Press, Incorporated
814 North Franklin Street
Chicago, Illinois 60610
First Chicago Review Press edition: 1990
Published 1967, 1969, 1970, 1973 by Brigham Young University Press, Provo, Utah
ISBN 1-55652-323-8
Printed in the United States of America
5 4 3 2 1

OUTDOOR
SURVIVAL
SKILLS

SIXTH EDITION

LARRY DEAN OLSEN

CHICAGO
REVIEW
PRESS

Library of Congress Cataloging-in-Publication Data

Olsen, Larry Dean, 1939–
    Outdoor survival skills / by Larry Dean Olsen.—6th ed.
      p.   cm.
    Includes index.
    ISBN 1-55652-323-8 (pbk.: alk. paper)
    1. Wilderness survival.   I. Title
GV200.5.047 1998
613.6'9—dc21

                                                97-20442
                                                CIP

Published by Chicago Review Press, Incorporated
814 North Franklin Street
Chicago, Illinois 60610
First Chicago Review Press edition: 1990
Published 1967, 1969, 1970, 1973 by Brigham Young University Press, Provo, Utah
ISBN 1-55652-323-8
Printed in the United States of America
5 4 3 2 1

To my ancient fathers, who lifted their voices of counsel in the dust of my walkings and upon the breezes.

To all the Native American people, past and present, whose history and culture stirred the curiosity of my youth and guided my footsteps in the path I have walked. My esteem for the indigenous people of the Americas developed as I studied, duplicated, and implemented the tools, skills, and ways of the Ancient Ones.

Few people revere Mother Earth as do the Native Americans. They endeavor to live in harmony with nature and the elements of wind, rain, and fire. Their past sufferings, tears, and dreams are written on the sandstone walls of time. Their future greatness is also written by the Creator on tablets of gold. Mother Earth loves the Native Americans. She has provided them with all the necessities of life. This book attests to that reality. It is to these, the First Americans, that I dedicate, with love and respect, this thirtieth-anniversary edition of *Outdoor Survival Skills*.

The author and his family, 1967.

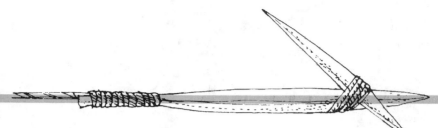

Acknowledgments

My wife, Sherrel, has cooked my meals for many moons in caves and under open skies; raised my children in freedom; and put up with my wandership. L. Paul Newman, Jim L. Winder, and Robert L. Burnham camped with me in the early days of my makings. Richard A. Olsen and the late Albert Taylor taught me as a boy. Ezekiel Sanchez, my friend and partner, cofounded with me the Anasazi Way, which has produced a "change of heart" in the lives of thousands of young Walkers. Patricia Slafter, Dave Holliday, David Wescott, Jim Riggs, Bart and Robin Blankenship, Nikki Purcell, Janet Schurz, Fred Bohman, Suzanne Herman, and a vast host of Trail Walkers have field-tested skills and endured many miles of Stone-Age wanderings. The Anasazi Foundation people live today with young people on the trail in the Anasazi Way. Dan Smith, William Whitiker, Ural Lathan, Evard Gibby, Pauline Sanchez, and Scott Pentzer have helped with and supplied pictures and sketches. My many children have lived the primitive lifestyle as a family and have taught me patience and how to love. To all of these and to the more than twelve thousand young Walkers who have lived the skills of this book, thanks.

Contents

From left: Ezekiel Sanchez, Larry Dean Olsen, and L. Paul Newman.

Foreword to the 1997 Edition

Thirty years ago, in 1967, the publication of *Outdoor Survival Skills* made a powerful impact on a world of varied interests in self-reliant living. It entered a world of cold-war basement bomb shelters, a world of social psychology and social experimentation where reality therapy was forming the foundations of tough love. Individual and group empowerment through the elevation of self-esteem was acquiring broad acceptance. Sensitivity training, out of which emerged individual and team problem-solving through confidence games and "ropes courses," was just beginning.

Larry Olsen and *Outdoor Survival Skills* made an indelible mark on that world. First of all, the book featured a completely self-sufficient approach to the problems of survival living. It employed and taught the fascinating arts of the best survivors in the world's history—the Native Americans and the aboriginal tribes of all continents.

Indeed, because of his "no kit nor any premanufactured items" approach, Larry Olsen won the confidence of a nation of romantics and ended up at the forefront of what became a great movement to research and revive the arts of stone, bone, wood, water, and earth skills. He initiated a forum for rendezvous gatherings where those who had mastered primitive arts could gather periodically to teach and learn from each other. From these forums emerged dozens of authors and a public information base that is a repository for primitive methodologies that for centuries endured as mysteries passed verbally through the generations but never written down.

Larry Olsen went on to author a wilderness survival merit badge for the Boy Scouts of America. He authored a significant revision of the U.S. Air Force's survival manual and was a technical consultant to Robert Redford in the production of the movie *Jeremiah Johnson*. He has written numerous articles and traveled the United States widely, consulting and lecturing.

Secondly, Larry won the confidence of a community of adventure-seekers who immediately employed him to conduct extended expeditions into the wilderness to prove the efficacy of the skills he taught. Today a number of the nation's finest schools for wilderness survival are conducted by his former students.

Thirdly, Larry's groups discovered that living primitively for an extended period becomes a powerful life-changing experience. One could not live for a time in the Stone Age and ever again look upon the Space Age in the same light. The life-changing quality of an expedition with a Larry Olsen group caught the imagination of the world of psychological counseling and therapy. Larry and his associates have spent thirty years establishing programs and consulting with programs in the western United States; today he is the recognized pioneer/progenitor of western primitive wilderness therapy. It is a matter of historic record that a Larry-Olsen–administered program has never suffered a death, nor an incident of life-endangering neglect, nor an incident of dereliction or abuse.

Perhaps in this third area Larry Olsen will make his most consequential contribution. Since 1988 he and his longtime associate Ezekiel Sanchez have established and operated the Anasazi Foundation in Mesa, Arizona. Anasazi is a model adolescent wilderness treatment program. In 1996 it was the first of its kind to obtain national accreditation from the Council on Accreditation of Services for Families and Children. During its eight years of operation it has served thousands of client families with a perfect safety record and outcomes that more than double the national averages for treatment of adolescent issues.

Larry has been active as a board member and advocate of the National Association of Therapeutic Wilderness Camps. He has filled leadership roles on committees to establish and promote wilderness program ethics. His guidance is sought throughout this industry for methods of nonconfrontive and nonpunitive stewardship over adolescents in wilderness settings. Dr. C. Terry Warner has given his methods the name "agentive therapy." Larry is describing and articulating this therapy in a new book, *The Anasazi Way*. In 1996 he joined with Warner and others to launch the formation of Family Works, a nonprofit nationwide effort to share the harvest of his thirty years of experience along with the lifework of Dr. Warner in communicating principles of moral agency, changing at the heart level, family harmony, and community interdependence.

Perhaps the finest tribute one could offer this remarkable pioneer would be to observe that he and his wonderful companion of thirty-seven years are the natural parents of six sons and four daughters and the foster parents of more than a dozen children. This thirty-year anniversary edition of *Outdoor Survival Skills* is but one testament to Larry Dean Olsen's many contributions to the world we all live in.

—L. Paul Newman

given us a truthful and interesting documentation of an early lifestyle in America. His knowledge of a man's conditioning to snow and the high country as well as to heat and the barren desert is enormous. As an actor, I am very concerned about detail and authenticity, and I am comfortable that the accounts of an early lifestyle in this film are accurate. Mr. Olsen's tireless efforts and superior ability have made this possible.

—Robert Redford
Warner Bros. Studios
Burbank, California

Ezekiel Sanchez.

Prologue

The Philosophy of a Caveman

It is asserted from time to time that true survival is measured by a person's capacity to stay put and prepared with a super pack of hauled-in safeguards; that learning edible plants and trapping and hunting skills are not necessary since most lost persons are rescued within seventy-two hours anyway. Without negating the wisdom of preparation and safeguard, I would say that the philosophy behind this modern dependency is still a dangerous one. Because of confidence and practice, when one learns to live off the land entirely, being lost is no longer life-threatening. Any manufactured item, such as a good knife or sleeping bag, then becomes a useful and appreciated luxury, but not a dire necessity!

Example: On a particularly dry day, Zeke Sanchez stepped from a small boat onto a bleak stretch of the shore of Lake Powell in southern Utah. The man who owned the boat and had given us the ride across the lake stared open-mouthed as Zeke handed me his gear and bade me farewell. He was on his way to catch up with a group of students and leaders about three days ahead of him in some of the most beautiful but forbidding desert land in North America. He was dressed in jeans, boots, and a long-sleeved shirt, and on his head was tied a large bandana. That was all. The boatman called out to Zeke, "What about your pack?"

"He doesn't want it," I interrupted. "He needs to travel fast to catch the group before the week is over."

"But. . . but he can't live out there without *something*!" said the boatman. "What about a canteen, a sleeping bag, and something to eat?"

"He knows where the water is, he sleeps on a coal bed, and the roots are easy digging," I assured him.

Zeke disappeared over the first sand ridge of Iron Top Mesa and the boatman took me across the lake, talking all the while of unsuspecting individuals who had died in that very desert. He was certain Zeke was a dead man. I quietly acknowledged his concern, and agreed with him that the desert is indeed a dangerous place. I said even if a person is "prepared" with all the freeze-dried, super-lightweight, ripstop finery that technology offers, it's still dangerous. The desert has a way of getting "things" away from you. Still, without technological carry-ins, a person might not survive; that is, most people might not survive.

Fig. I. The author straightening an arrowshaft.

Fig. 2. Sharpening a stone knife.

Fig. 3. Using a flint knife.

Fig. 4. Starting a fire with the bow drill.

Although the boatman was wise to the harshness of the land and was a veteran of many desert travels and even rescue operations, he had little confidence in his, or anyone's, ability to make it out there without some basic camping and survival gear.

Zeke, on the other hand, was not oblivious to the reality of the desert. Instead, he possessed a oneness with that land and knew how to use what was already there for survival. Zeke might have enjoyed a sleeping bag, but he was not bound to it, and traveling quickly was more important in his mind. Since he had poked his nose into many crevices in times past, he knew how and where to look for water rather than scenery, so he was outfitted completely.

In the wilderness, one must realize that there is not a single condition of extremity that is entirely without purpose. Every hour is beneficial to those who make it their study and aim to improve upon the experience they gain. What becomes a survival situation to one person may not concern another. Besides, who can count on being rescued within seventy-two hours? It's just not a very personal statistic!

Three days later, Zeke caught up to his student group, well watered and sassy from eating pack rats, cicadas, mahonia berries, biscuit-roots, *Chenopodium*, and cactus fruits. He sported two new ratskin possibles pouches, a woven rice grass sleeping mat, a greasewood digging stick, two dozen Paiute deadfall triggers, firesticks, twenty feet of cliffrose rope, a jasper knife, a bone weaving awl, an unfinished serviceberry bow stave, and a whole bundle of reed grass arrowshafts.

Survival studies have shown that those who adapt successfully in a situation of stress share some attributes that set them apart from those who don't adapt. A survivor possesses determination, a positive degree of stubbornness, well-defined values, self-direction, and a belief in the goodness of humankind. He is also cooperative. He does not feel that humanity's basic nature is to promote only self-interest; instead, he believes that most people are concerned about the well-being of others. Consequently, he is active in daily life and is usually a leader, though he may also belong to groups as a strong follower.

A survivor is also kind to himself. He does not fear pain or discomfort, nor does he seek to punish himself with them. He is not a self-hater. Even the most difficult existence is acceptable to him if it is beyond his ability to change it. Otherwise he will fight for change. He knows the odds.

Fig. 5. Using a pump drill.

Because a survival situation carries an aura of timelessness, a survivor cannot allow himself to be overcome by its duration or quality. A survivor accepts the situation as it is and improves it from that standpoint (Figs. 1-5). One of civilized humanity's greatest weaknesses is the inability to do this easily. If punching a timeclock improves efficiency, it may conversely jangle a person's ability to endure to the end—that is, if he lets it.

A survivor also possesses a utopian attitude. This does not reflect an orientation toward comfort but an artistic ability to make even the most miserable existence seem like millennial splendor. I have witnessed this in my best students. Their digging sticks are works of art, their deadfalls ingenious, and their camps miracles of compactness and industry. There is nothing crude in the primitive existence of these people.

Stone Age living implies two things: first, an immersion within the affective domain of life, and second, a life centered away from comfort and ease. Affective living places much of the meaning of life in the world of work—of doing. Priorities in a hand-to-mouth existence quickly force industry to an exalted plane. If they did not, existence would become unbearable. Activity and industry merged with increased spiritual insight form a union that may preserve life beyond the normal limits.

Life on a higher plane than comfort and ease may seem strange in our culture, but it is an important quality of people who survive. This point has grave consequences for the comfort-oriented individual lost in the wilderness. In Utah a man once died of dehydration beside a desert stream because the water was uncomfortably dirty.

Time is life, and where existence is reduced to a hand-to-mouth level, comfort must take a second seat. In survival terms we might say that comfort only gets in the way. A strong person may die of exposure if he neglects himself, but he may also die if he babies himself.

Lessons of survival learned in a classroom or laboratory setting may be helpful, but they will never replace direct application. My own experience has taught me that it is possible to rise above the comfort-seeking level in a primitive situation and establish priorities that not only insure my survival but grant me the added qualities of confidence and serenity as I attempt to exist in my environment. Even when the going gets rough and death becomes a grim possibility, that confidence and serenity never leave; thus struggles become challenges and my mind is better able to function without fear or panic.

I am reminded of the man who, alone in a vast desert with no hat, no water, and a broken leg, pulled himself up on one bruised and battered elbow and smiled at a bunch of dry grass, saying, "You know, if this keeps up I *might* get discouraged."

Through the years I have presented the challenge of primitive survival to several thousand students. Under some of the toughest wilderness conditions these students have tramped hundreds of miles across rivers, mountains, and deserts of the West. There is no question in my mind that young people today are as tough as their pioneer forebears. However, the most disturbing discovery of these expeditions has been the types of stress that cause people to give up. Many students drop in their tracks, not from physical exhaustion, but from mental anguish. They are often afraid to make the effort once they realize the magnitude of the challenge.

Then there is the other extreme—those who at first appearance seem unable to make it but who plow through to the end despite their physical limitations. They have their minds set on success. Incidents from two expeditions illustrate this positive stubbornness in a survival situation.

John was overweight and a slow hiker. He found the pace exhausting and breathing difficult in the intense heat of the desert. Water was scarce and the small group of students was bent on pushing to a small seep spring some twenty miles away. Worried, I assigned two students to hang back and keep an eye on him. Two instructors, in good shape, pushed ahead, running, with instructions to bring back water for the stragglers.

At the seep spring, several hours later, I was surprised to hear that John had made it completely on his own. To top it off, he had assisted one of the students assigned to him in bringing in another student who had sprained an ankle. They came in singing.

During the weeks that followed, John became the physician of his group and spent hours helping others. He made the three-hundred-mile trek and never required more than his share of the meager food and water.

On another expedition, we had been three weeks on the trail, our destination taking us into the wind, which was blowing in the first winter storm. The terrain was steep and broken. The advance scout returned with word of a large overhanging cliff that would shelter the whole group until the storm passed. It was located about eight miles away near the top of a high ridge, and we began heading for it just as the sun went down.

We had been several days on meager rations and water, and many of the students had bad blisters, which was par for any course of this kind. Our food supply consisted of a bag of flour and some Brigham brush (*Ephedra*) for making a warm drink.

The first group to reach the cave built a fire and rolled up in blankets to sleep, too worn-out to eat. A short time later three more exhausted students came in with word that six others were having a rough time about three miles from the cave, halfway up the steep hill. The rest of the students were struggling up in small groups.

By this time it was dark, the wind had increased to a gale, and snow was falling. I found the group who had arrived first at the cave arguing with the three who had brought in the report. The newcomers wanted the others to help make Brigham tea and ashcakes (flour and water patted into small cakes and baked in hot ashes) to take back to the struggling students below. The arguing proved futile, so the three alone prepared about fifty ashcakes and warm Brigham drink. Then one stayed at the fire cooking more food while the other two went back down the mountain with food and drink to aid the six laggers.

By two o'clock A.M. they had brought in the last of the group, fed them again, and stacked a huge pile of firewood. They warmed cold feet, doctored blisters, and cheered hearts as best they could under the circumstances. Zeke Sanchez, one of those three students, became a leader of many desert treks.

1

Old Badger and me.

The Badgerstone

As a boy I was filled with desert things. Beyond the green of hay fields, in a land of sand and sage, I sifted artifacts of clay and bone and stone and ancient ways, filling my imaginings with adventures, digging secrets from rock shelters and caves. I recovered the cry and mighty thrill of the chase and the taste of broiling meat. I found the chill of winter and starving and the blast of summer's alkali wind. It was all mine, the Anasazi Way—a new way to "the making of a being." I was hearing a new voice from the dust.

The tones of flaking flint and the crumbling metate humbling seeds into small ashcakes stirred up desire in me to survive, to master some skills of the Ancient Ones. I stepped far from bicycles and baseball into the making of a long walking.

After many years, I sat on a rock and wrote the first edition of this book. I gathered about me many Walkers wanting to make a living off the land and wanting to use Stone Age tools for making it. Awakenings happened that transformed me. They came in events of discovery: the blinding whiteness of sunbaked eyelids; the sight of perfect growing edibles; the arching curve of my sleek rabbitstick; the flickering heart of my precious prey; the darkened dust of countless cooking hearths; generations of stone, bone, and fiber; the satisfaction and warmth of fire.

The book flew through many good editions. Now this thirtieth-year publication celebrates some early events and feelings and shares a few tales of how I learned the Anasazi Way and the making of these survival skills.

The badgerstone changed my life forever. It all began when I was twelve years old.

In the Beginning

Miss Romain wanted my eyes on the blackboard, but out the window and westward across the desert lay the cave, and my eyes saw only the treasure in its deep floor. On Tuesday, I started making a new pair of high-topped moccasins from an old pair of field boots. I cut off the soles, turned the boots inside out, and started sewing on soles of cowhide leather.

On Wednesday I rolled up a blanket pack, sharpened my pocketknife and a small hunting knife, and made a long possibles bag from the leg of an old pair of Levi's. I filled it with survival supplies: fishhooks and line, bandages, matches, notebook, pencils, two muskrat traps, a roll of waxed linen string, three apples, one large onion, three potatoes, three carrots, a poke of salt, a small canteen of water, three dry biscuits, and one Hershey bar (in case of emergency).

By midnight I had the soles stitched on my moccasins and a long piece of clothesline rope tied onto my blanket roll. I was ready.

My mother had watched my preparations carefully and had suggested enough additional gear to fill a covered wagon. I told her I wasn't going clear to Oregon. "Besides," I said confidently, "you're lucky I'm even taking this stuff. If I really went whole-hog Paiute, I'd have to go naked, 'cept for my moccasins, 'cause they're the only things I have that's real Indian."

Actually, field-boot moccasins were only part Indian; the part where I did the stitchings myself. Momma sort of nodded a vague understanding of my plans. She understood my need to go. Skipping school for important projects like this one wasn't against her personal plans for my success in life. Daddy wasn't too concerned about my schooling either, but he had plenty to say about me going into the desert alone. After two days of stern warnings on everything from mosquitoes to rattlesnakes, he ran out of advice. On Thursday morning he drove me to the west desert and left me there. I later learned that he followed me for the first mile just to see if I was really serious.

My trail led down a steep gully for the first two miles. From that point I climbed up a long side canyon to the bluff above. The desert stretched flat to the horizon. In the distance there appeared a thin dark line that I took to be No Name Creek Canyon. I headed for it with a sure expectation of a powerful adventure. This was my first solo expedition. I had absorbed a great deal of interesting facts about Paiutes, Anasazi, and the flora and fauna of the great plateau deserts of Idaho. As yet this potful of facts had been tested only in my mind, aided by the breezes. I was counting on my instincts to bring me success. My father did not know just how far I planned to hike. Actually, I hadn't realized it myself, and I wondered right off if I could get there and back to the drop-point by Saturday evening.

I had previously spent parts of days alone working on Uncle Bill's farm and several one-night camp outs in the desert by myself. As I hiked along the flat, three days seemed like quite a big chunk of time in this unknown, roadless place. But the land felt good under my new moccasin soles, and each step brought me more and more in touch with the breezes. I walked and tossed between a tiny grip of fear and a peaceful blending with the desert.

Sage grew skimpy and short. Scattered on the flats were countless red-ant mounds, each surrounded by circles of bare earth where the ants had stripped the ground around their little pyramids. As I walked along observing each ant mound, a general pattern began to emerge. The ants had constructed their rounded mounds with one side a bit steeper than the others. This steep slope was almost always facing south, southeast. At the base of the steep side was their entrance hole. I noted in my journal that the few exceptions were due to some natural obstruction on the south side of a mound, like a tall bush or rock that shaded it. From this observation I concluded that the ants depended on the sun to warm their lives each day, especially in the winter when the sun swung low along the southern horizon and the ants were deep below the frost line. The steep exposure sucked up heat, which reduced the grip of winter cold on the mound. I knew that ants remained active all winter. They stored food all summer long in anticipation of the cold times. Now I had discovered they also built heat-efficient housing. I wondered what else these little tribes of desert dwellers could teach me. I thought about the story of the Ant and the Grasshopper, and I thought about my parents and our grocery store and the prophet who taught Mormons to store food and fuel for two years ahead.

Somehow, I couldn't relate the ants to Miss Romain's class at school. I wondered whether ants found it necessary to hold classes of instruction for all upcoming antlets in order to maintain their organized and busy mound-building society. Red ants seemed ever ready for a fierce fight, though, so maybe they did have a school of some sort after all.

Finally it struck me that the ants could serve as well as teach me. No longer were those little creatures mere teachers of philosophy, social organization, and architecture. They could also be my professional guides as I hiked. It was so very simple. At any time of the year, whether cloudy or in blizzard, the little mounds, averaged together, faced south. I knew then that I would never lose my way in the land of red ants.

Red ants were also troublesome. The flat stretched on and on and despite my many new thoughts and discoveries, the desert heat began to press down upon me. I had to move faster toward the still-thin rim of No Name Canyon.

The stitching broke slowly at first. Then, stubbing against a rock, the whole right-toe end tore loose and started flopping. My once-pleasant walking on the new soles of my moccasins suddenly became agony as my right foot scooped up sand and stickers and worst of all, red ants. I hobbled on, fighting back the new urge that came strong upon me with each step. Then the big toe on my left foot poked through and I tripped along in double-plop in the middle of nowhere. My feet were fairly tough and the sand didn't bother me too much, but the stickers and red ants soon found the tender spots between my toes. Finally I stopped, sat on my blanket roll, and pondered my dirty feet with little red pricks and bites all over them. They looked wholly unsuited for this terrain. In just four miles of hiking, my Paiute stitching had failed me. Now I was totally un-Paiute and miserable. The canyon rim looked even farther away and I wondered if I had been walking backward or something. I drank some of my water and slumped in the dirt on the big flat in the miserable west desert.

Going back seemed the only way for me. The treasure was far away and the vision was fading. I drowsed in the pungent shade of a sagebrush for a few minutes, and as I lay there, all my thoughts disappeared. The vision was gone. The sky was white in the heat and alkali dirt parched my lips and tongue. The quiet settled in all around me. I could feel the thump of my heart as it performed its duty without any effort or desire on my part.

Slowly, I felt thumpings coming through the ground under me. In time with my heartbeat filtered a rhythmic pounding in the soil. I felt it in the ground around me, but I could hear nothing. In the stillness there came a sense that I wasn't alone out there after all. Was it some-one walking? Indians could hear the cavalry coming every time they put their ears to the ground. I just lay there, straining.

In a few minutes, I heard a muffled growl and a spitting noise. It was really close! I sat up and turned toward the sound. The hairs on the back of my neck prickled. There was a small mound of sand just behind my shade bush. The bush was blocking my view, so I carefully crawled about three feet and peered over. Less than five feet away was a large hole dug in the ground. It was almost big enough for a boy my size to crawl into. Sloping upward away from the hole was a ramp of dirt tail-ings that peaked sharply at its top, clearly testifying to the enormous amount of earth moving that had taken place there.

The muffled growls and hissing were coming from the hole. Then a furry rump emerged. It was a badger, a big one, coming out of the den backward!

My curiosity faded as fear swept over me. I was too close. Every boy in southern Idaho knew that badgers didn't back down from a fight. They chased worse than cactus. I was barefoot; no chance to outrun this monster. Right then I wanted someone to appear and rescue me. I almost cried out, "Momma!"

The badger was growling fiercely and hissing. I could hear my heart right between my ears.

Old Badger came out of the earth and backed up the long dirt ramp. He held in his front claws a fist-sized stone, dragging and rolling it along up the ramp. His flat body topped the ramp and pitched awkwardly down the other side. This brought the stone to the top of the mound, but it slipped from his grip and went rolling back down the ramp and into the hole. Old Badger seemed to realize the failure of his attempt to remove the pesky stone. He let out a low growl and thrashed a bush near his nose, where I lay low. Old Badger finally lumbered back into the ground grumbling and hissing with typical badger temperament. I had my chance to slip on my broken moccasins and get out of that place, but I didn't. Old Badger hadn't seen or smelled me on his first trip out of the hole. Maybe I could watch for awhile. I could hear him deep underground almost beneath me, spitting and struggling.

Presently Old Badger's rump emerged and once again he backed up the dirt ramp, pulling the stone along. Once again he backed his flat body over the crest and lost his grip on the stone. It rolled back down the hole. Old Badger spat out a whole string of unique sounds and followed the path of the stone back into the ground.

The badger and the stone repeated the same dance over and over again until I became weary of watching. His situation seemed hopeless, with the ready-made ramp and track for that stone to roll back on. His only hope was to keep a hold on the stone. This he seemed unable to do once his body tipped over the crest of the dirt mound. I wanted to crawl over and give him a hand.

Then, on about the fourteenth attempt, Old Badger held onto the stone and pulled it over the crest. It tumbled down the back side away from the hole. Old Badger just sat there and rested for awhile. The growling and hissing stopped. He seemed really pleased for a moment.

Then I got nervous. So taken was I by the drama of the badger and the stone that I forgot how dangerous badgers were and how very, very close my nose was to his. The sudden tension I felt must have caused a movement or a vibration that reached the senses of Old Badger. He rose up and our eyes met. His nose sniffed me out, but he didn't bristle. I almost fainted. If he chased me, he would catch me. I knew it. We stared at each other for a long moment. Old Badger made the first move. Without any show of anger or bluff he gave me a nod, a last blink, and slipped smoothly down the ramp into his new den. I could feel him digging new ground below me. Then I realized that my heart had stopped pounding and I felt warm, at ease, and somehow very privileged.

I slipped on my torn moccasins, picked up my gear, and started to leave. I glanced back at the hole and noticed the stone the badger had struggled with so long. It was cleaner and smoother than the rough native lava of the area. I stepped quickly over to the dirt mound, picked up the stone, and walked quickly away from the badger's den. To my surprise it turned out to be a broken half of a well-crafted Indian mano, or handstone. I could smell Old Badger on it. I held it in my hand for a long time before slipping it reverently into my possibles bag. I spit right into the breeze and pointed my tattered toes westward toward the ever thickening black line of No Name Canyon. I plopped along for almost a mile before realizing that my despair and give-up-itis was completely gone. My feet still suffered from the loose stitchings in my moccasins, but not unbearably as before. What had happened? What had Old Badger done to make such a change in the way I felt in this harsh and endless desert? Had I been taught by an animal? Truly this had happened, and a surge of genuine toughness flowed through my whole body. I was Badger Clan.

2

The finest wickiup.

Shelter

The Finest Wickiup

It took all day to cut the willows, haul bundles of long dry grass to the site, and carefully and with much love ply the grass in neat layers to form our first wickiup. Bob Burnham and I had completed the finest grass-thatched shelter ever made by fourteen-year-olds! The moment demanded a celebration. Bob jumped on his horse and sped away to retrieve two ducks from our river camp. We would eat a feast in the new shelter.

Inside the wickiup, I tended a small fire and slowly built it up so a hot bed of cooking coals would be ready when Bob returned. We had placed all our gear inside and there was still plenty of room for two to stretch out on each side of the firepit. Outside, patches of snow cooled the breezes, but none of it reached through the thick grass matting of the structure. I felt secure and safe. I stretched, placed a few more sticks on the fire, closed my eyes—and dozed.

A brisk crackling in my ears woke me and immediately burning bits of grass fell all over me. Our beautiful wickiup burst into brilliant light. I was lying at the back and the doorway was aflame as well as the whole front slope clear to the top. My heart jumped and I plunged headfirst right through the side of our carefully and lovingly laid wickiup wall. I rolled into a snow patch, slapping and yelling at burning bits of my clothes and hair.

Fig. 6. Brush and bark wickiup.

It only took seconds for the wickiup to reach a peak of flame and heat enough to ruin most of our survival gear. My bow and quiver of arrows were toast. Our blankets and extra clothes were singed through. In the distance I saw Bob riding hard, with the ducks flopping from his belt. I stood helpless as he pulled up, breathless and wide-eyed. "Still want to celebrate?" I asked lamely.

Shelter Basics

One of the first outdoor skills a person must learn is how to construct an adequate shelter. He must know what type of shelter is most appropriate for a given situation and understand that the techniques used for building it depend upon need and time. Most shelters should be built according to a few basic specifications; however, special circumstances such as rain or snowstorms or extremely cold weather may dictate any kind of makeshift protection that can be built in a hurry. Nevertheless, after a degree of protection has been achieved, a semipermanent shelter should be constructed to assure safety in the event that conditions get worse.

Building for survival requires more than a minimum of effort and calls for sound planning. Most essential to this planning is the selection of a campsite. A good campsite provides the following necessities:

- Protection from wind and storms.
- Protection from flash floods, rock falls, high tide.
- Freedom from poisonous plants, insect pests (ants, mosquitoes, fleas), and harmful animals.
- Level ground for a bed and fireplace.
- Access to materials for making a shelter and a bed.
- Adequate firewood.
- Access to food sources and drinking water.
- Dry ground located away from creek bottoms and green grassy areas.

A good firepit is also essential to survival. As it is used primarily for heating and cooking, it should be

- at least eight inches deep and lined with stones.

- surrounded with spark protectors, which can be made from green pine boughs or upright sticks. (If the protectors stand at least six inches high, most popping sparks will be stopped.)
- placed in a direct line with the shelter entrance and slightly forward from the center, as this allows ample space at the back of the lodge.

Also of major importance in building for survival are the dimensions and strength of the shelter. It must

- allow free movement around the fire.
- provide space for a dry woodpile just inside the opening.
- provide plenty of storage for food and gear.
- allow for a fair-sized firepit for cooking and heating and enough space from walls and ceiling to prevent flames and sparks from catching in thatch materials.
- be strong enough to withstand high winds and heavy snowfalls (Figs. 7, 8). (There is nothing quite like having your shelter fall in on you at three o'clock A.M.)

The construction of the shelter should include the following:

- Strong supporting poles lashed firmly, although most other poles and thatching can be laid on without lashing.
- Heavy branches stacked against the finished lodge to prevent the wind from scattering the thatching when it is composed of grass and boughs.
- Plenty of matting and grass for a floor covering, which must be kept at least one foot away from the fire and stirred up each evening, or, even better, removed completely from the shelter and then respread — especially important in snake country.

Lean-to

Easy-to-build windbreaks serve well for summer living and give ample protection in cold weather if sturdy (Fig. 9). However, they are only temporary emergency shelters. When constructed, a lean-to should provide protection from the prevailing *night* wind, contain a large reflector so that maximum heat can be obtained from the fire, and be three-sided so that maximum protection can be obtained.

Fig. 7. Framework for large shelter.

Fig. 8. Heavy thatching for sturdy shelter.

Fig. 9. Three-sided lean-to.

Fig. 10. Wickiup.

Fig. 12. Large wickiup.

Fig. 11. Reed grass wickiup.

Brush Wickiup

A good wickiup takes only a little longer to build than a lean-to and is more serviceable (Figs. 6, 10). This comfortable dwelling is one of the best, as it provides protection from all sides. It consists of a tripod on which a tight circle of poles is stacked to form a large tipi or cone-shaped frame. Over this frame is placed a thatching of brush, leaves, reeds, bark, rotten wood, pine boughs, and even dirt (Fig. 11). The entrance can be large and face the rising sun, or it can be small and provide protection from all outside breezes. Using twenty-foot poles, one can make the floor space fourteen feet across, providing sleeping space for eight people (Fig. 12). These rough shelters protect from wind and cold but are not generally effective in a prolonged rainstorm. More sophisticated methods are needed for a truly waterproof shelter. A pole or grass-thatched wickiup will do the job.

Pole Wickiup

In heavily timbered areas, large wickiups can be built to house several people and their gear. Gather all the dry, dead poles and long sticks in the area. Erect a three-pole tripod in the same manner as a tipi (Fig. 13).

With the tripod in place, carefully lay on successive poles, insuring that the spread is even and smooth. No poles should stand out from the

Fig. 13. Pole wickiup.

rest. Trim poles of their branches by knocking these off with a club. As the poles are laid on, the space at the top of the tripod will fill up. Shorter poles can be placed in the remaining spaces, and the wider spots near the base can be filled in with shorter slabs of bark, split wood, sticks, and short poles. The point is to fill in all the spaces with something solid.

The next step is to apply a layer of boughs, grass, and plant stalks over the outside, stuffing materials into the cracks and spaces. Start at the base of the frame and layer the covering, overlapping each tier as you go up the sides of the frame. To reach the top half of the wickiup, construct a single-rung pole ladder and rest it against the frame.

When the grass and bough covering is in place, start again at the base and cover the entire wickiup with an additional layer of mulch and dirt. This will stop even a driving rain and make the shelter cozy and durable for a long period of time. It takes awhile, but it is well worth the effort. To gather the mulch, select areas under large trees where the forest floor is deeply matted with pine needles, leaves, and vegetable matter. Dig out the mulch in layers, if possible, and haul it to the wickiup site in blanket bundles. The mulch can be laid on shingle-fashion or packed thickly against the sides at the base to insure a solid base to build on. Make sure the mulch cover is thick and well packed.

The final step is to keep the mulch from blowing away by applying a last layer of poles, branches, and sticks to the outside. Just lay them against the wickiup to hold everything in place.

The final product should be a solid structure with a small entrance facing east or southeast. A firepit is made in the center of the inside circle, and a good layer of dry grass is spread for bedding. I have built these wickiups in many areas, and they have survived several winters of heavy snow, providing shelter for animals as well as humans.

Grass-Thatched Wickiup

A more permanent desert campsite deserves a unique and efficient home made of grass. It is easier to build than one might think, and when finished, it will withstand wind, rain, snow, and even cruel desert heat. However, fire has its way with this shelter, and constant care must be taken to prevent flying sparks.

To build a grass wickiup, first secure three sturdy poles in the ground with the ends almost touching at the top. This is best done by scratch-

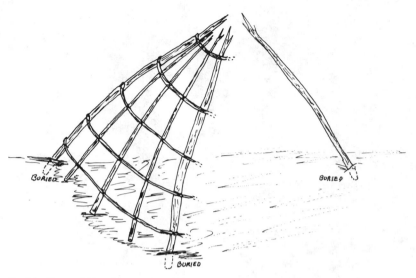

BURIED

BURIED

BURIED

Fig. 14. Grass wickiup frame.

ing a circle for the wickiup on the ground and digging the postholes at least eighteen inches deep and an equal distance apart around the circle. Solidly tamp the backfill around each post with a heavy pole. This tripole frame provides the support for the whole structure.

With a hard wooden stake, pound additional holes in the ground every twelve to fifteen inches around the perimeter of the circle. Insert long trimmed willow poles in the holes to form a full frame structure (Fig. 14).

With long willow withes, bind the entire frame together, beginning about fifteen inches from the bottom with the first round. Then add successive rounds about fifteen inches apart clear to the top of the frame. The withe rounds should be tied to each pole in the frame. This can be done with green strips of willow bark, cattail leaves, sagebrush, cliffrose bark strips, or any other natural cordage (Fig. 14).

It is important to construct the frame with all parts evenly spaced so that no frame poles protrude out from the cone surface or sag inward. This will not only look better but will insure a proper lay for the grass thatching.

The next step is to harvest great armloads of long dry grass. Cut the grass in bunches or simply pull it out in hand-sized clumps. Be sure to stack each armload evenly with all the root ends together. Neatly tie each bundle to prevent the grass from tangling and mixing during

Fig. 15. Making grass thatching.

transportation to the wickiup site. Sometimes you have to range out for several miles to gather enough good grass. There are several varieties of tall desert thatching grass, including bunchgrass, crested wheat, wild rye, and even June grass. The best long grass grows on steep slopes and at the base of cliffs. It is usually found lying flat in mats, pressed down from winter snow. Try to harvest only dry grass that was growing the previous season. Older grass stalks are often brittle and rotted. Green grass works well, but it must be dried before use.

Carefully separate the grass into small bundles about one-and-one-third to one-and-one-half inches in diameter, with all the root ends together. Two strands of cordage are used to tie the small grass bundles to each other in a kind of "hula" skirt (Fig. 15). The first course of cordage starts about four inches from the root ends, with the second course being tied on at the same time approximately four inches up the bundles from the first cord. Each course is tied with a simple half hitch or, if desired, with a twined weave (see Weaving, in Chapter 7). The twined weave is less secure but easier if you are using bark cordage.

Make the skirts from two to four feet long for easy handling. Roll them up and set them aside until you have enough completed to make the first course around the base of the wickiup.

Fig. 16. Rod Allred by his grass thatch wickiup.

Fig. 17. Grass thatch wickiup.

To lay on the first course, select a space for the doorway. Face the doorway to the east, southeast, or south, depending on the time of year. Summer doors face east and make shade out front during the heat of afternoon. Winter doors face south and catch the sun most of the day. Starting at the selected door pole, tie the skirts in place every twelve to eighteen inches along the frame. The ties can be secured to the pole frames and also to the circular withes of the frames. Make sure the grass skirt tips are resting or pressed tightly against the ground all the way around the wickiup. Bank a little dirt against them on the outside, or lay some short pieces of wood against them at ground level.

When the first tier or course of grass is secured on the frame, take slender willows and tie them on the outside all the way around the base of the skirts. Tie each withe securely through the grass thatch to the frame poles. A small sharp stick will poke the holes necessary to thread the cord through the grass.

Construct the second course of thatch and place it on the frame in the same manner, making sure that the skirts overlap almost half the length of the first course. This insures a tight covering. When the skirts are tied in place, run another course of willow withes around the outside, this time making sure that they hold down both the top of the first course and the overlapping second course. This construction will withstand strong winds (Figs. 16, 17).

Continue laying on courses of thatch until the top of the shelter is reached. The upper tiers are best worked on with a single-rung ladder on the outside, and something to stand on inside the shelter.

Leave the very top of the wickiup open for a smoke hole and build a small hearth near the center of the inside circle. From the inside, fill any cracks or holes with strips of loose grass and remove any hanging strands that might catch in the fire or tickle the back of your neck.

A covering for the door can be made by making an extra skirt of grass with three or more strands of weave. It may be secured to a willow frame if desired.

Living arrangements in a grass wickiup require some basic etiquette and a lot of caution. Keep all bedding materials securely away from the fire. This can be done with small poles or stones framing the beds. Keep the ground around the fire free of straw, twigs, or any burnable materials. Never step across the firepit. Dragging feet will pull combustible materials into the pit, and they may burst into flame when you are gone. It is best never to leave a flaming fire burning unattended in a shelter. From experience I can say that after many hours of hard work building a warm wickiup, the last thing you want is to see it lighting up the sky.

Rock Shelter

The favorite natural protection of the Native Americans in the West was the rock shelter, an overhanging cliff or bank that affords protection from the elements (Fig. 18). With a minimum of effort these shallow caves can be turned into first-class living quarters.

In the winter, rock shelters facing south catch the sun's warmth most of the day. For added protection, low windbreaks or reflectors can be built across the front of the cave. Poles leaned against the outside edge of the roof and thatching, as in the construction of a wickiup, constitute a cave shelter that can be completely sealed from the elements.

Fig. 18. Rock shelter (cave).

Fig. 19. Insulated wattlework.

Insulated Wattlework

A little more time and patience is needed in the construction of a wattlework shelter, but the comfort it provides is worth the extra effort (Fig. 19). Each wall is made with two parallel rows of stakes driven into the ground about a foot apart. Willow sticks are woven between the stakes to form a fairly tight mesh, and grass and other materials are stuffed between the two woven walls. The result is a thick, insulated wall that will stop any cold. The roof is simply made of poles and willows with grass thatching piled on top. Heavy willow rods and brush are piled on top of the grass to keep the wind from blowing it away.

Sweat Lodge

The Navajo Indians make a small earth lodge for sweating purposes, but it also serves as a warm shelter (Figs. 20, 21). Simply a small wickiup covered with a thick layer of dirt, it should be built over a pit large enough to accommodate at least one person and a firepit. The earthen

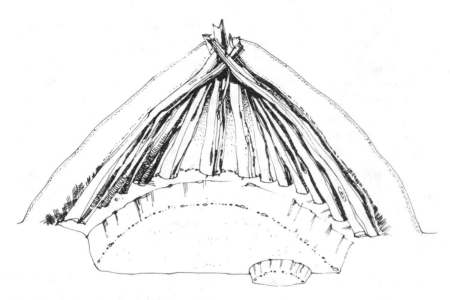

Fig. 20. Cross section of sweat lodge.

Fig. 21. Finished sweat lodge.

covering should seal off all areas where air might enter. The entrance must be small, just large enough for a person to crawl into, and should have as tight a covering as possible.

For warming this shelter a large fire must be built outside the entrance and several rocks heated. A small pit dug inside and to the left of the entrance serves as the heating pit. A person sitting inside can reach out through the entrance with a set of wooden tongs, pick a hot rock out of the fire, and pull it in, making sure that all the sparks and coals are shaken off. A single rock in the pit will heat the shelter for several hours. When it begins to cool, it can be replaced by another rock from the hot bed of coals outside.

Snow

Snow caves are simple to construct, as they are merely dug into a snowbank that has a good crust, but they are not generally warm (Figs. 22, 23). If well built, however, snow shelters can be heated adequately; but if they are to be comfortable, a lot of matting and floor covering is necessary. Lean-to shelters and wickiups covered with snow are excellent.

Snow Cave

Traditional shelters of snow are at best chilly tombs to ward off more severe cold and provide emergency protection from the wind and storm. Seldom is a snow cave suitable for comfortable housekeeping on a long-term basis unless elaborate preparations and special construction techniques are used. When the problem is survival, however, even the damp and cold of a snow cave are inviting compared to being out in the open.

In recent years many methods and styles have been tried, tested, and evaluated. Perhaps the most efficient system is one suggested by Ernest Wilkinson, a veteran wilderness guide in Colorado. With consideration for area and snow depth, I have used the following method successfully.

Select a campsite away from potential avalanche or snowslide paths. Be sure there is plenty of firewood available. Within this site, select a large, deep snowdrift that has crusted over. Tramp down a good camp space in the front or lee side of the drift. Build a firepit and a fire and pile up a snow windbreak on either side of the campsite. Stack firewood for outside cooking and warmth.

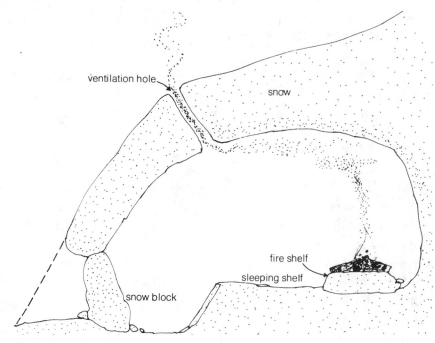

Fig. 22. Snow cave.

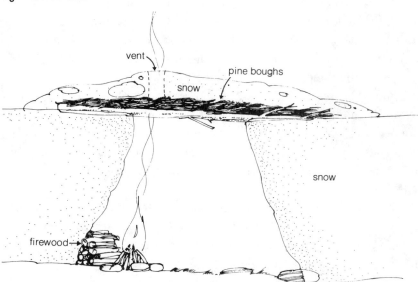

Fig. 23. Snow pit.

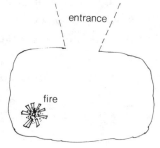

Square off the front of the drift and begin digging a hall tunnel big enough to walk into, but sloped upward as you go. If possible, cut the snow out in chunks. (A good knife can be made by flattening a long stick into a blade.) Make the tunnel about four feet high for easy standing room and about two and one-half to three feet wide. Tunnel in eight to ten feet if possible.

Once this initial hall tunnel is completed, construct sleeping bunks on either side of the hall. To do this, cut out the snow, beginning about two feet inside the hallway and continuing all the way to the back of the tunnel. Make the shelves at least two and one-half feet wide and as high as possible above the sloping tunnel floor. This way the heat will circulate high around the sleeping shelves, while the cold air sinks in the hallway. The ceiling should be shaped into a dome, and the snow roof should be at least a foot thick (Fig. 22).

The entrance to the tunnel at this point is wide-open, with easy access for construction, but it lets the wind blow right in. It must be sealed off. Before doing this, however, haul in all your gear and bedding materials and some small pieces of firewood. Place several inches of insulation—pine boughs, dry grass, sagebrush tops, juniper bark, and so forth—on the sleeping benches, along with whatever blankets, pads, or sleeping gear you might have. Another good insulation is a row of sticks two or three inches in diameter lying side by side crosswise on the sleeping benches, covered with pine boughs. At the back of the hall tunnel, construct a separate shelf for storing gear and pad it also with branches and other insulation to keep the items from coming into direct contact with the snow.

When all the gear and bedding are in place, use the snow blocks excavated from the tunnel to rebuild the entrance. Completely seal it up and pack the cracks with snow. After it sets up for a few minutes, cut an entrance hole just large enough to crawl into. The hole should be low, near the floor of the tunnel, so that the heat, which rises, will be trapped inside the shelter around the sleeping benches. A loose piece of cloth or a pile of pine boughs can be placed in the hole after you are inside for the night, to break any wind blowing in, but the hole should not be sealed off completely.

It is not necessary to build a large fire inside for light and warmth. If a candle is available, that's all you need. Lacking candles or lamps, a fire can be built but kept very small. Make it on top of a tin can, in a tin

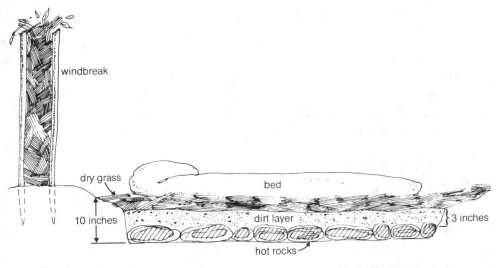

windbreak

dry grass

bed

10 inches

dirt layer

3 inches

hot rocks

Fig. 24. Hot coal bed.

Fig. 25. Hot coal bed lined with stones.

Fig. 26. Removing ashes from heated bed.

cup, or on a small, flat rock, and feed it with shavings and small twigs. In any case, create a draft for the fire by poking a small hole through the ceiling of the snow cave. Eventually the ceiling will glaze over from the heat and the shelter will cease to "breathe." The entrance and the smoke hole in the ceiling will help keep the air fresh and clear of smoke.

Matting and Bedding

Sleeping in some degree of comfort is an important part of the shelter and can be achieved rather easily. Dry grass, pine boughs, sagebrush bark, cattail stalks, bulrushes, and reeds make excellent bedding and can be found at any time of the year. In the winter, dry grass is located at the base of cliffs that face south. Snow usually melts away in these areas and the sun keeps the grass dry. Rats' nests that contain enough grass for bedding are usually found in cracks and small caves, but they may contain cactus spines as well.

Hot Coal Bed

Heated ground under a bed makes even the coldest nights comfortable. But care must be taken not to allow direct contact with the hot stones. Even after several hours of cooling, the rocks will still burn holes in bedding. After the stones are heated by a fire built right in the pit, the ashes that have accumulated are scraped out before the covering of dirt is applied (Figs. 24–26).

The Making of a Squirming, or How Not to Sleep on a Hot Coal Bed

From the river we followed Zeke back across the flat and made camp against a large sandstone cliff, which offered some protection from the elements and put us away from the stinking river. The cliff faced southeast, with a gentle sand swell sweeping away toward the flat from its base. Zeke climbed to the top of the swell, searched briefly in the sand, and picked up an agate chip and a broken piece of ancient pottery.

"My people slept here in times past. We camp here," he said.

"Yeah, but," said one of the students in a tired voice, "it looks much better down there on the flat where the grass is."

Zeke hung his gear in a juniper and squatted in a teaching position on the top of the swell.

"This place rises above the river bottom. In the night, cold air will sink below us onto the flat, and it will be warmer here. The cliff will greet the morning sun first and reflect warmth to us early. The cliff behind breaks the night breezes from the west."

"But the wind is out of the east today," said Tim. "It will blow right on us all night."

Zeke winked, but ignored the statement. He continued, "If rain falls, we can find shelter under the overhanging cliff. There is juniper wood here and much tall dry grass nearby." Looking beyond the students, he pointed to the grassy flat and said, "Most campers choose a green spot on the riverbank for their camps. They rig up modern miracle models of civilization to scare off the dampness of the grass, the cold air from the river, and the mosquitoes. They sleep in, waiting for the sun, which shines there last and leaves there first."

Several nodded in innocent appreciation, showing some excitement at the thought of sleeping in such a wonderful place as the sand swell by the cliff so far from the river.

"The east wind will bring us a storm in a few days, but at night it dies and the breezes follow down the canyons until the sun brings back the east wind. Here the night breeze will come from the west."

With that we turned our attention toward the approaching night. Zeke, in his usual jovial mood, jostled the less eager members of our group who were standing around with their hands in their pockets. He herded them toward a gravel outcropping. Soon everyone began straggling back into camp toting bundles of firewood and cobble-sized stones from the gravel hill. We selected a broad sandy area where nothing was growing and scraped out a pit approximately six feet wide and long enough so that all the group could lie down side by side.

Zeke's boys, later known as the "blister patrol," helped their leader line the pit with the cobblestones (or rather, they watched him do it). Zeke placed each stone carefully. When this was finished, he instructed a group to pile sticks and brush over the stones in the pit. Then with a hot coal from the fire, he lit the pile of brush. In a few moments the whole sky was lit up. It took nearly an hour for the fire to burn down to a hot bed of coals. Upon this, we tossed smaller sticks and strips of bark to keep the fire going for another hour.

Meanwhile, some of the apprentice fire starters, who had returned from the sagebrush patch with enough potential to burn up the countryside, began sweating, grunting, and groaning as they tried to master the technique of keeping a spinning drill in a socket that wouldn't hold still under an unsteady foot. As it grew darker, these enthusiasts moved closer and closer to the hot coal bed, where they strained in the firelight to see and master the machines they had created.

I remembered the first time I had tried to start a fire with a bow drill. I had frittered away the daylight hours perfecting my shelter for that first night. When the darkness was upon me I had tried to control the rickety bow drill in the darkness and failed. So, shivering, I had tromped down a short track in the brush and spent the night running back and forth to keep from freezing to death. I have never made that mistake again, always starting my fire well before dark. Now, I thought how fortunate these people were who, in the presence of warming flame, light, and helpful teachers, were learning a softened version of my hard lesson.

Zeke finally pronounced the coal bed hot enough, and with long sticks everyone began scraping out the larger burning coals and embers, leaving a thin layer of ashes over the very hot stones. Then he instructed everyone to scoop up handfuls of dry sand from the surface of the ground, warning them not to scoop too deep into the moist sand below. They threw the dry sand over the ashes until they had built up a layer approximately ten inches deep over the stones.

By this time it was quite late and the rigors of this first day were beginning to show on everyone. I was conscious that no one had even mentioned eating.

Zeke went behind a bush and returned with a neat bundle of dried bunchgrass and cliffrose bark. He had gathered it earlier without anyone noticing. He silently and deliberately stepped onto the coal bed, opened his bundle, and spread out a soft straw cushion over the spot where he chose to lie for the night. There was a flurry of puzzled looks and confusion as everyone disappeared into the darkness to scratch up what they could for the night's bedding. Some returned with only a handful; others were more fortunate. Within the hour they all had a spot on the hot coal bed.

I waited until everyone was settled and then nestled on one end, next to Big Taylor. About that time Zeke arose from his warm bed and, grabbing his blanket, surrendered his spot to the person sleeping next to him, who gladly slid over onto his matting. This left a gap that was soon filled as each person shoved to the center in an effort to snuggle. The evening was becoming quite cool. Zeke ambled over to the campfire and plopped down. "Good move," I thought. "I should join him." But the coal bed was getting warm and I was comfortable. Though I sensed it would not last long, I closed my eyes and tried to sleep anyway.

It's a wondering sight, not to mention sound, to see a sleeping person suddenly rise straightupendicular, seemingly propelled by a force that leaves a trail of smoke and sparks; awake in orbit, ripping and tearing the air to shreds, to at last plop to earth with a bewildered, helpless air of embarrassment. I suppose my slumber has been interrupted in this fashion on at least a hundred previous occasions. Each time the cause has been identified without question—squirming. No other sleeping action could so interrupt a tranquil condition upon a hot coal bed. I can testify that only squirming produces such spectacular results.

Now Zeke had taken great pains to insure the proper depth of insulating dirt between the hot rocks and the bedding material of dry grass. Furthermore, the group had received an elaborate Zeke-type sermon on the virtues of not squirming. He had warned: "No hip holes on community hot coal beds! Moving around too much keeps the others awake. It also scrapes away the insulating dirt. Sardines never swim in the can!"

But sure enough, not an hour had passed before the center occupant levitated, releasing from under him that telltale smell of burning wool. He was lucky. The burn hole was only as big as a pumpkin and his hip was only first degree. Over by the fire Zeke rose up in a cloud of dust and, pointing a fierce finger toward the sky, mockingly and humorously tongue-lashed the whole group, repeating his earlier admonitions and throwing in a comment to the effect that civilization and soft beds had surely ruined these "gringos" for the good life under the stars and that he was certain that unless they all practiced better P.M.A. (Positive Mental Attitude) and quit squirming, chances were they would all be roasted and ready to eat before morning. Then with the air of a great chieftain, he pulled his blanket tightly around himself and dropped in the dust from whence he had arisen.

He was right. At midnight some guy near the middle yelled, "Fire!" Big Taylor beside me mumbled something about a steam bath, and the next thing I knew there was whooping all over the place, with sparks and smoke streaming in every direction. I noticed three or four red glowing patches of light streaking toward the river. Without any compassion

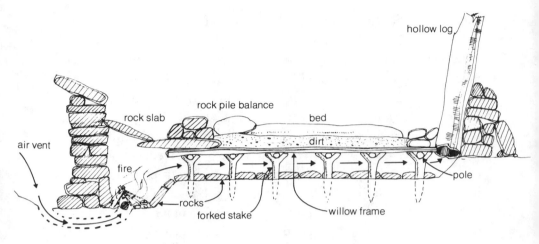

Fig. 27. Chimney draft bed.

Fig. 28. Stone oven.

at all I grabbed my blanket and stomped over to the campfire, curled up next to Zeke, and pleasantly cooled off for the rest of the night. Zeke never moved. I awoke once or twice to throw wood on the fire and noticed a lot of talking going on over at the coal bed.

Chimney Draft Bed

This bed is complicated to construct, but for any warm-bed enthusiast, it is unequaled for comfort in cold weather (Fig. 27). Such a bed is best constructed inside a large shelter or cave, since the bed itself provides very little protection from wind and storm. The elaborate chimney draft bed illustrated here (Fig. 27) has in recent years given way to a more efficient model, which can be built as follows.

Construct a stone and mud oven two and one-half feet in diameter and below ground level. Construct a door twelve inches in diameter at the base of the oven on the downwind side. This door will open into the flue trench and will enable you to feed the oven fire. Chink the stone with a mixture of mud and grass. As the dome goes up, place the stones so that they gradually pull inward. A green willow support frame on the inside will make this part of the job easy. Just below ground level, near the top of the dome, leave a hole about six inches in diameter at the point where the flue trench begins. The flue trench should be built downwind from the oven (Fig. 28).

Dig a trench approximately ten inches wide and six inches deep in a straight line eight feet long. Line the sides of the trench with flat stones to bring its width down to five or six inches. Then place wide, flat stones over the trench, completely covering it. Seal cracks and joints with the mud and grass mixture, making sure that none falls inside the trench (Figs. 29, 30).

Place two long sticks, logs, or lines of stones parallel on either side of the flue trench and about four feet apart if two people will be using the bed, or two and one-half feet apart if only one person will be using it. Stake the logs down so they won't roll away. Fill the space between the logs and over the flue trench stones with dry sand, dry grass, and boughs to a depth of about three inches.

At the opposite end of the trench, construct a stone and mud chimney to a height of not less than four feet, the higher the better (Fig. 31). Make sure it is airtight and sturdy, with an expanding base that covers the opening to the flue trench. The flue at the top of the chimney should be about six inches in diameter.

Build a small fire inside the oven to dry it out and expose any leaks in the oven, along the line, or in the chimney. Fan the fire by blowing through the oven door until smoke starts drawing through the chimney (Fig. 32).

Fig. 29. Building the trench.

Fig. 30. Covering the trench.

Fig. 31. Building the chimney.

Later, build a larger fire and keep it stoked until a deep bed of hot coals is formed in the oven. Fill the oven again with wood and place a slab of rock against the door, sealing out most but not all the air. This will act as a damper and keep the fire burning slowly for all-night comfort (Figs. 33, 34). A further refinement is to build an A-frame shelter over the bed. A person can sleep comfortably without even a blanket in this type of arrangement.

Group Heat Trap

Occasionally a group of people may be caught in the open. Usually the best plan is to keep moving, because hiking or other exertion maintains warmth. However, in cold, windy conditions, short rest periods are essential to regain strength. Ordinarily it is advisable to stand while resting to prevent muscles from stiffening and cramping. When distances are great, however, and longer rests are needed, it is wise to get into a more restful position as sheltered as possible from the cold or wind. Failure to

Fig. 32. Smoking chimney.

Fig. 33. Completed chimney draft bed.

Fig. 34. All-night comfort.

do this can result in a fatal loss of body heat. By forming a group heat trap or ground-level body shelter, people can trap a great deal of heat and maintain body temperature at a higher level while they are resting. One way to do this is as follows:

- Everyone sits shoulder-to-shoulder in a tight circle, pointing their feet inward.

- Each person sits on one edge of a blanket or sleeping bag or whatever covering is available and pulls the rest of it around his back and over the top of his head.

- Hold the blanket forward with the hands or tuck it under one foot to form a sort of sitting hammock. This will relieve the strain on the back from sitting on the ground and will form a canopy over the head.

- When everyone in the circle is doing this, a tight windbreak is formed with a semisecure canopy overhead to hold in the heat. It is surprising how much warmer this arrangement is than merely wrapping up and huddling. Each person can be watched carefully for signs of hypothermia and the group can talk, plan, or play games to take the edge off their harsh circumstances.

3

Fig. 35. Starting a fire with the hand drill.

Fire

First Flame

After a hundred tries, many blisters, and bruised knuckles, it felt right. The bow turned the spindle smoothly. My body felt the ease of the correct motion. It was a natural flow of movement as I crouched over the fireset. Smoke welled from the socket and grew persistent. I knew I had it.

For almost a year I had lived for this moment. I had seen a picture of a bow-drill set and read a story where an Indian had made fire with one. But without an example or firsthand view of the process, I had fumbled miserably with clumsy equipment—too large, too blunt, too slick, too crooked, and completely defiant of my expectations!

With the spark aglow in the tinder bundle and the sudden burst of flame, I realized what a simple thing it was to make a fire by friction. From that long-ago moment until this day, the power of fire has been mine, tempered by my location and the availability of fire-giving wood.

Spinning out a flame is more than a skill. It is the building of a relationship with the right wood, stone, and string and the giving of a special motion or life to the form of the fireset. Through the years, hundreds of first-flame makers have expressed to me the same feelings of immense awe and complete "being" that I experienced so long ago. No other experience is quite the same.

Fire Basics

The importance of a good fire can hardly be overestimated. Even in warm weather a fire is essential, not only for warmth at night but for cooking, signaling, purifying water, and aiding in the manufacture of various useful items. The following methods of creating fire should be studied carefully and practiced. Reading about how to start a fire without matches is one thing, but doing it is another.

An inexperienced person in the wilds without matches or other modern methods of making fire will find that primitive methods are beyond his ability. On the other hand, an experienced artisan may create a good fire in less than a minute, with only materials found in nature (Fig. 35).

Success in making fires is achieved only with practice and carefully wrought equipment. No amount of effort will produce a fire when dexterity is lacking and equipment is crude. Getting that first spark to burst into flame is a challenge, but from that moment it is almost certain that future attempts will be successful.

Tinder

Tinder is made from dry bark that is light and fluffy, and from shredded grass, dry moss, birds' nests, and various plant fibers.

The preparation of tinder requires special attention. It should always be finely shredded (but not powdered) so that the bundle is a soft, fluffy, fibrous mass that will not fall apart. Rubbing the bundle between the hands is perhaps the best way to make the tinder light and fluffy (Fig. 36).

The following list contains the more common tinders available in nature. Others may be found by experimentation in different geographical areas.

Barks

- Cliffrose (*Cowania*): shrub. Outer bark from trunk and larger limbs (colorplate 8).

Fig. 36. Preparing tinder.

Fig. 37. Making a nest in a tinder bundle.

- Cottonwood (*Populus*): tree. Inner cambium layer on old dead trees (colorplate 8).

- Sagebrush (*Artemisia tridentata*): shrub. Outer bark from trunk of larger plants (colorplate 26).

- Juniper (*Juniperus*): tree. Outer bark from trunk of mature trees (colorplate 15).

Plant Fibers and Silks

- Yucca (*Yucca*): fibers from pounded dead leaves or ready-made at the base of dead plants.

- Nettle (*Urtica*): fibers from pounded dead stalks (colorplate 20).

- Milkweed (*Asclepias*): fibers from pounded dead stalks; also silk from pods (colorplate 16).

- Dogbane (*Apocynum*): fibers from pounded dead stalks (colorplate 9).

- Thistle (*Cirsium*): down from tops (colorplate 30).

- Cattail (*Typha*): down from seed heads (colorplate 7).

- Various grasses: dead leaf blades, partially decomposed, lying at base of plants.

Flint and Steel

Steel, a luxury item, is rarely found in nature and then only if someone has left or lost it. When present in the form of a pocketknife, nail file, and so forth, it can be used in combination with a hard stone to produce sparks hot enough to catch tinder.

Flint stones come in a wide range of types, all of which contain some silica. Agate, jasper, and quartzite are perhaps the best, though any silica stone will do. It should be broken into angular chunks to produce sharp edges. The tinder bundle must be of the finest-quality material, sagebrush, cottonwood, or cliffrose bark being the best. A small nest is made in the tinder bundle and the finest-shredded material is loosely sprinkled in the depression (Fig. 37).

Striking the spark takes a little practice. The best method is to hold the stone in one hand and the closed blade of a pocketknife, or something similar, in the other, and with a rather loose-jointed-wrist approach,

Fig. 38. Striking a spark.

Fig. 39. Blowing a spark into flame.

Fig. 40. Bow drill.

strike the sharp edge of the stone hard until sparks fly off and fall onto the tinder bundle (Fig. 38). A thin wisp of smoke will signal that a spark has caught. Then the tinder bundle must be picked up quickly and very gently, and the spark must be fanned by blowing gently on it with short puffs of air. If the timing of these actions is just right, the spark will spread and burst into flame (Fig. 39).

A surer way of getting sparks to hold and catch is to use specially prepared charred tinder. Once a fire has been produced by other means, it is a simple matter to make plenty of charred tinder for quick, easy fires later on. Manure, wood punk, or pithy plant stalks are burned until very black and then smothered in an airtight container or simply stepped on several times in very dry dust. Plant stalks should be split to expose the pith. When charred, the material can be stored in small containers or wrapped inside tinder bundles until time for use. For best results, manure, punk, and pith should be crumbled into powder after charring.

A cotton handkerchief, a piece of cotton cloth cut from a shirttail, or any piece of cotton charred in the same manner is superior to punk or pith if it can be sacrificed. The charred cotton, once placed in the fire bundle, catches readily when sparks fall on it and holds longer than punk or pith. Excellent sources of materials for charred tinder are as follows:

- Masses of very soft dry rot found in rotted fallen logs of the cottonwood (*Populus*) and some other trees (colorplate 8).

- The pithy core found in the center stalk or spike of the yucca (*Yucca*).

- The pithy core found in stalks of mullein (*Verbascum*, colorplate 19).

- The large but rather tough pith found in stalks of elderberry (*Sambucus*, colorplate 9).

- The soft pith of the sunflower (*Helianthus*, colorplate 30).

- Manure, found in dry chunks in all areas frequented by livestock or game.

Bow Drill

Making fire with a bow drill is a simple matter if the apparatus is constructed correctly. The bow drill has four parts: a fireboard, a drill, a socket, and a bow (Fig. 40).

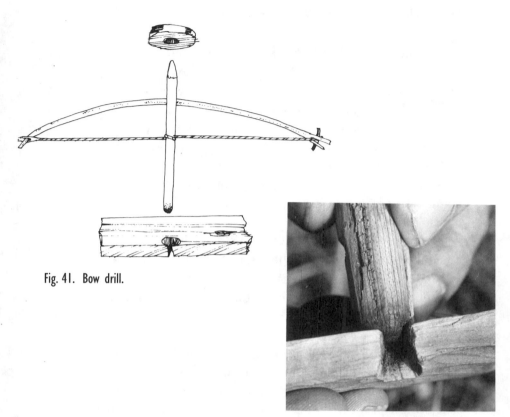

Fig. 41. Bow drill.

Fig. 42. The all-important notch.

Fig. 43. Getting a spark.

An excellent fireboard, which should be about one-half inch thick, can be made from a dead cottonwood branch. A slight depression must be drilled along one edge and smoothed and deepened by a few turns of the bow and drill. A notch that reaches to the center of the pith is cut in the side of the board. This notch catches the fine powder ground off by the drill. It is in this fine powder that the spark is formed (Figs. 41, 42).

The drill may be of the same wood as the fireboard and should be from eight to twelve inches long and about three-quarters of an inch in diameter. The top end is sharpened to a point while the bottom end is blunt.

The socket is made by drilling a depression in any piece of hardwood or stone that fits the hand. When in use, the drill runs smoother if the socket is lubricated with grease. Enough lubrication can be obtained by rubbing the top of the drill stick through the hair or on each side of the nose. Using water to lubricate a drill only makes the wood swell and bind.

The bow should be eighteen to twenty-five inches long and about one-half inch in diameter. A branch with a fork on one end makes an excellent bow. The best string is a strip of one-quarter-inch-wide buckskin or other leather, but substitutes can be made from plant fibers, shoelaces, or any other cord. The cord is attached to one end of the bow and twisted until it is tight and round before being tied to the other end. It is a good idea to fix one end in such a way that it may be loosened or tightened as needed. If the bow drill does not run smoothly, it may be that a little more twist in the cord is needed.

To use the bow drill, place the fireboard on a flat piece of bark or wood. The spark will fall onto this piece and can then be carried to the tinder. Another method is to dig a small depression under the fireboard and place the tinder in it, in a position where the spark will fall directly into it.

To work the fireset properly, get down on one knee and place one foot on the fireboard to hold it steady. Then place the drill, with the bow cord twisted once around it, into the fireboard socket. Using the hand socket to apply pressure, move the bow back and forth in a sawing motion with steady, even strokes until the drill tip is smoking well (Fig. 43). Gradually spin the drill faster and apply more pressure with the hand socket. After a lot of black dust from the drill starts collecting beside the notch and there is plenty of smoke, there should be enough

Fig. 44. Lifting the bow drill from the socket.

Fig. 45. Placing the spark in tinder.

Fig. 46. Blowing the spark into flame.

heat to create a spark. Lift the drill away carefully and fan the pile of black dust lightly with the hand. If there is a spark, the pile will begin to glow. When this happens, the spark must be placed carefully into the tinder and blown into a flame (Figs. 44–46).

Hand Drill

Making a fire with a hand drill is considered the most accomplished fire-making talent. As a method, it is worthy of all serious people of the wilderness. Having mastered the bow-drill set, you have reached the next step, where the bow and hand socket are replaced by well-earned calluses on the palms of your hands. In the making of this learning, expect blisters.

At the annual Rabbitstick gathering (for more information, see Author's Note, p. ii), many "abo people" spend their time twirling sticks to accomplish a hand-drill fire. It is surprising how many make it!

Without a teacher, I spent years experimenting, giving up in total frustration only to be drawn back to the challenge later. I learned that the selection and preparation of materials are critical. Patience and a steady stance is the next part and can only be arrived at with a feeling for the fire hiding in the set.

Fig. 47. Using the hand drill.

A good hand-drill set consists of a spindle from twelve to sixteen inches long and a little larger than the diameter of a pencil. It should taper slightly from the drill tip up to the top. The drill should be made of a soft, pithy wood such as cattail stalk, yucca, arrowweed, beargrass stalk, seep willow, and so forth. Or a more solid shaft can be fitted with a softwood tip. Excellent drill tips are made of sagebrush, yucca, and cottonwood.

The fireboard is similar to the bow-drill board, but can be much smaller, with holes and notches in proportion to the size of the drill tip. The notch for hand-drill boards should be narrower than that for bow-drill boards.

Spin the drill in the palms of your hands, starting at the top of the spindle. As you spin, your hands will tend to work down the shaft. As your hands near the lower end, smoothly yet quickly let go, raise your hands to the top, and start over again. It is OK for the drill to stop during this "changing of the grip." Practice will develop a style suitable for you. Some devotees are able to spin the drill by rotating their palms in a circular motion as they spin, thus preventing their hands from working down the drill so that there is no pause in the drilling (Fig. 47).

Other Methods

Various other techniques can be used to make fire, including the fire saw, in which two sticks are rubbed together in a notch until a spark is formed; the fire thong, in which a strong vine or rope is pulled back and forth in a split stick; and optics, in which a lens from glasses, a flashlight, field glasses, the bottom of a pop bottle, or a bottle filled with water is used to concentrate the rays of the sun.

Maintaining a Fire

Once a fire is made, precautions must be taken to keep it going. If you are camping in one spot for a period of time, you can keep a fire alive through the night by building up a deep bed of hot coals and banking them with ashes and a thin layer of dirt. The important thing is to keep the wind from the coals.

Tinder can be prepared for traveling purposes from shredded bark that is baked until it is powder-dry. It can then be carried in a dry container or wrapped in several strips of bark. The Paiute Indians ingeniously

Fig. 48. Fire bundles (the top bundle has been burning six hours).

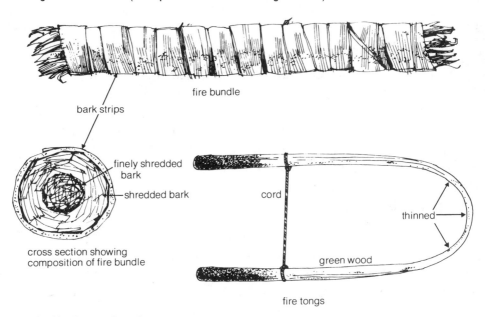

fire bundle

bark strips

finely shredded bark

shredded bark

cross section showing composition of fire bundle

cord

thinned

green wood

fire tongs

Fig. 49. Fire bundle and tongs.

transported live fires over long distances by making a long bundle out of a core of shredded sagebrush or other bark placed on several thicknesses of dry stripped bark. Additional layers were placed on top and the whole bundle was wrapped tightly with more bark strips. When finished, the fire carrier looked like a giant cigar about two feet long and four inches in diameter (Figs. 48, 49). A hot coal was placed in one end and the Paiute traveled with the fire carrier in his hand or stuck in his belt. Such a bundle would hold a live spark for six to twelve hours. Usually two or three bundles were made and carried. When one burned low, the traveler stopped and built a small fire, and in a few minutes he had a new supply of hot coals from which he would light another bundle.

Miscellaneous Hints

- A fire blower for stirring up dead fires can be made from any hollow stem. Canary reed grass and elderberry stems are excellent.
- Flames should be used for boiling and baking and coals for broiling and frying.
- Split wood burns better than whole chunks or logs.
- A log will burn in two; therefore, there is no need to chop it.
- Softwoods give more light than hardwoods.
- Reflectors should be used for warmth.
- Fire tongs save scorched fingers.

4

Thirst.

Water

Thirst

We could smell the river long before we could see it—eastern Utah's San Rafael was running thick with gypsum-grey alkali, pushed along by late-season mountain thunderstorms and minifloods beginning miles to the west. The land around us was drought stricken. In our desert canyon the sky was clear and it was hot.

At the river, our group dug into the banks, letting the water seep and filter through the sand to fill our holes. But it was no use. The filtered water still stank, and those who tried it vomited within minutes.

We camped dry that night with a hope that the water seeping through the bank would settle and clear by morning. Just in case, I organized the group into small parties who would begin to search for water at first light. One party would search the white sandstone swells for "pothole" or "tank" water. Others would search the side gullies and cliffs for seep springs.

Most of the group seemed to handle going to bed without a drink quite well. As for myself, I suffered. The others had eaten and drunk their fill just prior to joining me that day. I, however, had already spent two and a half months on the trail. That morning I had hiked eighteen miles alone to greet this new group of eighteen Walkers with their four instructors. The trek had been long and dry and my body was already on the edge of dehydration. The Walkers had hiked about three miles from the drop point near the river, none of us realizing that the flow had suddenly become poisoned. I felt I had made a bad mistake in pushing so hard and starting this group in new country.

In the morning our water holes still reeked of gypsum, so everyone was anxious to begin the quest for water. Each party fanned out to its assigned area. I joined a small group under the direction of Janet Simonson, a veteran instructor and daughter of the Shoshone tribe. She was well acquainted with hard times on the trail. We spread out in a large fan, walking up the gentle slopes of the white sandstone swells. These bare stone areas typically channel snow and rainwater into cracks and rivulets that join each other in deeper cracks, falling over small ledges to form deep rounded potholes or tanks in the solid stone. Some of these tanks, if shaded and deep enough, will store clean water clear through the dry months. Some hold hundreds of gallons. Others hold only quarts. Except for drowned lizards and insects, this water is clean and pure, generally the best to be had in canyon country.

My energy was very low, and I walked slowly with my arms limp, conserving what calories and moisture remained in my body. No one was to my right. Janet was in sight several hundred yards to my left. I spotted a likely-looking gully and headed toward it.

It is difficult to recapture or describe what it is like to just dry up and lose the function of arms and legs. Remembering is limited to brief seconds spread between long moments of semiconsciousness. At some point I stooped to pick up an old whisky bottle left by some long-ago sheepherder. The cap was still on the empty bottle. Then I remember whiteness; brilliant whiteness, and the ground around me faded and disappeared. I took a few steps and fell on my face. I wondered why I didn't put my arms out to break the fall. My face hit the slick rock and I felt blood but no pain. The bottle smashed to pieces under me.

My legs and back were sliding along, scraping against stone and brush. My right arm was stretched tight in the grip of someone dragging me in short jerks.

Then there was a slight shadow and I felt myself being propped up. I opened my eyes to whiteness, but I felt I was in the bottom of a gully, partly in the shade of an overhanging ledge. A few feet from me I could hear digging, in a low spot near the ledge. The ground was damp. I raised myself up a little, but I had no strength.

Slowly, as my sight returned, I saw Janet, digging with her bare hands, reaching into the hole up to her shoulder. I noticed the bottom half of the broken bottle standing near the hole. The cap was there, too. Whiteness overtook me again.

Someone was forcing the bottlecap between my lips, and my muddled brain was aware that a small amount of tepid water was trickling into my mouth. More capfuls followed. I vomited, and Janet forced more water into me. I started feeling really sick. Every part of me woke up and rebelled. My muscles cramped, my eyes ached, and all my innards seemed to twist at the same time. I could feel my heartbeat, magnified and fast. I didn't want any more water! But Janet forced me to keep drinking a capful at a time. Gradually I realized that she was bringing me back from severe dehydration.

In the next few hours, others helped me walk slowly back to camp. One of the groups had found a seep spring, and soon water was plentiful.

In the late afternoon a cowboy rode through our camp driving six head of cows. He said the water in the river was so bad that the cows were sick and going blind. He was evacuating. My group was refreshed and ready to push on to higher country and good water. I was still near delirium and couldn't go on, so the cowboy offered to take me out to a town where we could find help. I was put on the horse behind the man and my wrists were tied to the sides of the saddle. My head bounced against his back for the next three hours, until we reached his camp. From there, he drove me to a town, where I received medical treatment. They told me to eat and drink hearty and put a lot of salt on my food before I hit the trail again.

Three days later, I caught up with my group. Now we were all in good shape.

Water Basics

The Mountain West is often the scene of tragic experiences involving lack of water. But with a little luck and training anyone should be able to obtain enough drinking water to stay alive. There are areas, however,

Fig. 50. Water pockets—an easy-to-locate source of water.

that require special equipment if water is to be secured, for much of the desert area of the Great Basin is devoid of running water. Sources can be located without too much trouble if a person knows how to look for them (Figs. 50, 51).

Most of the moisture available in an area of dry mountain ranges can be found on the sloping side of hills. The other hillside is usually a steep escarpment and has faster runoff and less ground area for the collection of water. Narrow canyons and gullies should be followed up to their heads because small seeps and springs are often located nearby and run only a short distance before drying up.

The water table is usually close to the surface and can be located by digging as follows:

■ At the base of cliffs and rocks where an unusual amount of vegetation is thriving in dry mudholes, sinks, riverbeds, and the bends of riverbeds, the latter usually providing the easiest source of water.

Fig. 51. Drinking from a pool of water.

Fig. 52. Finding water at a depth of ten inches.

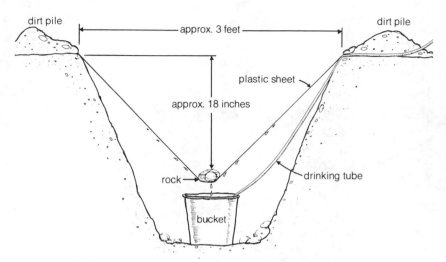

Fig. 53. Cross section of an evaporation still.

- At the base of large sand dunes on the shady or steep sides anywhere the ground is damp or muddy.

- In low spots where patches of salt grass, cattails, greasewood, willows, or elderberries grow.

- Where ore dumps and tailings indicate that water might be nearby in old mine shafts and pits.

Getting Water from the Soil

Obtaining water from the soil involves a few techniques with which anyone going into the wild should be familiar:

- A hole dug in damp or muddy sink areas allows water to seep in and collect (Fig. 52).

- Mud wrung in a shirt or other cloth will force out water.

- An evaporation still—an invention developed by two American scientists, Dr. Ray D. Jackson and Dr. Cornelius H. M. van Bravel of the U.S. Department of Agriculture—involves some special equipment but is simple to construct (Fig. 53). A sheet of six-by-six-foot clear plastic, a plastic drinking tube, and a container are all that are needed and can be included in a survival kit. A drinking tube is attached to the container—usually a bucket—and the container is placed into a hole dug three feet deep. Then the plastic sheet is stretched over the hole and held in place with dirt, which seals off the hole from the outside air. Next a rock is placed in the center of the plastic to weigh it down until it comes to within about two inches of the container rim. The drinking tube, placed inside the container, is arranged so it extends outside the still.

Two of these stills in operation in even the driest deserts will produce enough water daily for one person. Green plants and sliced cactus placed in the pit will increase the amount of water. It is best to place the still in old riverbeds or in deep, rich soil at the bottoms of gullies, where moisture is most plentiful.

Some people have been unsuccessful in their attempts to secure water with an evaporation still. At least one group has gone public with its failures, suggesting that the principle was not sound. One look at their research examples, however, reveals that their methods were at fault, not the principle.

Collecting Water from the Air and from Plants

Water can be extracted from almost any green vegetation by using a modified evaporation still. A large plastic bag is filled with vegetation and placed as in the illustration (Fig. 54). This arrangement is limited to the amount of vegetation you can handle at one time, but it may

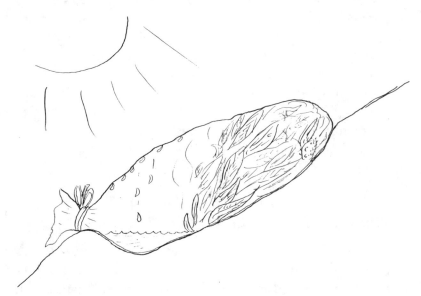

Fig. 54. Modified evaporation still.

Fig. 55. Dew available in early morning.

produce adequate supplemental water for survival. It is a good idea to crush or cut up the vegetation for quicker release of its moisture.

In many arid regions of the world, primitive peoples supply themselves with water by arising before dawn to mop up the dew from rocks and plants. A person using this technique in desert areas can gather a large supply of dew in the early morning (Fig. 55).

The easiest way to gather it is to use a handkerchief or a shirt to gently mop it up and then wring it into a container. If a handkerchief or other cloth is not available, a handful of dry grass will do the job. It is possible to mop up almost a quart an hour using this method.

Many plants and trees contain enough water to allay thirst, but getting it is a problem. A cactus can be cut and peeled and the moisture sucked out, but this is not the same as drinking running water; it is more like drinking white glue. However, larger cacti in the Southwest can be a good source of water when the tops are cut off and the center pulp is mashed and stirred with a stick. The pulp can then be wrung to obtain the water.

Collecting Water from Water Pockets

In the Southwest, much of the desert is made up of uplifted sandstone ridges or folds that sometimes run a hundred miles or more and completely dissect the land areas into separate valleys and drainages. These

Fig. 56. Narrow canyons—source of water pockets.

Fig. 57. Water pockets formed in sandstone.

exposed areas of stone absorb very little moisture, and a light rainstorm or snowstorm can cause considerable runoff, which in turn cuts deep channels and scoops out pockets in the surface. These pockets are numerous but extremely difficult to find, and as a result a person must ignore his basic instinct, which causes him to look in the lowest parts of a valley for water, and instead seek the high ground, where the water pockets are located. Side canyons, narrow clefts, and especially white sandstone ridges are the areas that should be carefully checked (Figs. 56, 57).

These hidden pockets may hold water for several months after a rain. In fact, some pockets are actually large tanks holding hundreds of gallons, while others are very small, holding a few quarts.

I have traveled with survival students as far as two hundred miles on foot across southwestern deserts without a canteen, relying mostly on these water pockets and a few small springs and seeps. Some stretches, to be sure, are completely devoid of water, but by carefully studying the terrain and sandstone formations, we have always been able to prepare a route and cross these areas to water-pocket country on the other side.

Precautions in Using Water

A person inexperienced in the outdoors will want to be thrifty in his use of water and will benefit from the following suggestions:

- Nothing should be eaten if water is not available. Eating uses up the body's water reserve.

- Water should be stored in the stomach and not in a canteen. People have died from dehydration with water still in their canteens.

- Water polluted by animals or mud tastes bad but is harmless if boiled.

- Muddy water can be partially cleared by allowing it to stand overnight, run through several thicknesses of cloth or a grass filter, or seep through the bank into a hole dug about a foot away. If the water is brackish or salty, the top six inches of salty soil between the hole and the source of water should be removed before the water is allowed to seep into the hole.

- There should be no traveling during the heat of the day and walking should be done slowly, not in a hurry.

- Such things as pebbles in the mouth, small sips of water, and chewing gum may relieve thirst, but they do not stop dehydration.

- The drinking of blood or urine increases dehydration of the body. But soaking clothing in urine is helpful, as evaporation from the wet clothing cools the body.

5

Fig. 58. Grinding sunflower seeds on a metate.

Plants

The American West is certainly no Garden of Eden with respect to food plants, but the variety available is extensive enough, and anyone with a good understanding of harvesting and preparation methods can live off these plant resources (Fig. 58).

It has been said that a person who can survive in the Great Basin can survive anywhere in the world. Portions of it surpass the hot barrenness of the Sahara, the cold ruggedness of Mongolia, and the jagged steepness of the Alps. But in all of these areas, nature has provided adequately for the trained survivor. The food quest is exacting and strenuous, and knowledge of the plant life is a must, as so many edible species resemble poisonous ones. A careful study of these plants is essential.

Moreover, a person must be aware of the impact he himself can make on a wilderness environment, especially on pristine desert lands. Some plants are becoming rare as their habitats are destroyed by agriculture and urbanization. Some plants need several years to grow large enough to harvest, and one meal could require several plants, perhaps the number found in about an acre of land. For example, one person could easily gather all the sego lily bulbs that occur in an acre or two of natural grassland for only one meal. Plants that produce an edible crop that can be harvested without destroying the plant should be used whenever possible. In other words, the trainee should exercise his "ecological conscience."

A certain amount of tastebud training, which comes from experimentation and determination, is often necessary before one finds some of these plants palatable. One should taste wild foods often and with a positive attitude. Many people die amid plenty because they cannot "stomach" wild foods. In these cases the stomach is reacting to the stimulus of a prejudiced brain. Some people even develop defense mechanisms against eating certain foods. Needless to say, these defenses can kill even a healthy person who is lost in the wilds.

Harvesting Food Plants

Roots

Finding an edible root is fairly easy, but most roots grow deep, and digging them out can be difficult unless one is prepared with a few good techniques. Skillfully applied, a simple device called a digging stick saves time and energy that is otherwise expended by scraping and grubbing with flat stones and fingers (Fig. 59). The stick is made from a stave of hardwood about three feet long and one inch in diameter. After the bark is removed, the stick is hardened in the fire and the tip of it rubbed into a chisel shape on a coarse rock. Green wood hardens after about four or five scorchings in the fire, but several scorchings are required to drive out the sap. Care must be taken that the wood does not burn, for a good fire-hardened stick must be baked, not charred.

Digging down to a tasty root involves moving a lot of dirt, and the digger finds that it is easier if he makes the root come to him. He can do this by pushing the stick down alongside the plant until it is even with or below the root. Then by slight prying but mostly lifting, he can flip the root to the surface (Fig. 60).

Seeds

When seeds are ripe, they can be gathered in large quantities with a seed beater and a gathering basket. The seed beater is a small woven dish or ladle used to knock the ripened seeds from the plants. It should be dish-shaped so that it can catch and propel the seeds into the basket.

Fig. 59. Digging with a digging stick.

Fig. 60. Proper use of digging stick.

The basket must be large enough to catch the seeds, yet small enough to be held in one arm. A shallow woven tray is ideal, but a shirt held open with a willow hoop will also work.

Plants that form large quantities of seed in clusters, such as amaranth (*Amaranthus*), can be stripped of their seeds with the hand. Flower seeds such as those of the nutritious sunflower (*Helianthus*) can be beaten from the head with a seed beater or picked by hand or rubbed from the head on a flat stone (Fig. 61).

Preparing Food Plants

Roots

Flour from roots can be made by drying and grinding the roots on a metate in much the same manner as seeds are ground. A metate is a slab of rock that has been smoothed. Roots may be roasted whole and eaten like baked potatoes or mashed on a metate and eaten like mashed

Fig. 61. Rubbing seeds from plant.

Fig. 62. Lining a steaming-pit with stones.

potatoes. Roasting, baking, or boiling may be used for most roots unless leaching is necessary to remove their bitter taste. Bitter greens, roots, and nuts such as acorns are leached by boiling them in several changes of water or by pouring hot water through a bag of the mashed food. However, this process takes away much of the food value of plants and should be used only when the food is otherwise too bitter to be eaten.

A steaming-pit is the most effective way to cook roots and greens, as well as meat and other foods. The pit is lined with stones and a fire is built in it. After an hour or more, the coals are scraped out and the pit is lined with wet green grass. The food is then placed on the grass and covered quickly with more wet grass. Next, water is poured on the food to induce steam, and the pit and its contents are quickly covered with flat rocks or a piece of cloth, canvas, or hide. Dirt is then heaped over the entire pit to seal in the steam, and the food is allowed to cook in the pit for several hours. One advantage of preparing food in this manner is that its flavor and nutritional value are preserved (Figs. 62–64).

Fig. 63. Preparing the pit for grass and food.

Fig. 64. Applying a dirt covering to the pit.

Roots and berries can be dried for future use. The roots are cooked and mashed into small flat cakes and then dried on flat rocks until hard. Berries must be partially dried first and then mashed into cakes for the final drying by being pounded in a mortar, or they can be mixed with pounded meat to make pemmican. However, these dried cakes must be broken or ground up before they are added to stews.

Seeds

Seeds must be threshed and winnowed if most of the chaff and stems are to be removed. One can accomplish this by beating the seeds with sticks and then tossing them on a winnowing tray, letting the wind blow away the chaff. This ancient method may seem rather crude, but it is effective under limited conditions. Seeds may also be tossed in a blanket or tossed into the air from a pile on the ground. A blanket or tray

Fig. 65. Beating seeds.

Fig. 66. Winnowing seeds by tossing.

saves many of the tossed seeds from being lost in the dirt. One can win-now small amounts by taking a handful at a time and blowing away the chaff while pouring the seeds from one hand to the other (Figs. 65–67).

Most seeds are tastier and more nutritious when ground into flour or cracked for mush than when eaten whole. A most valuable method of making flour or cracking seeds involves a grinding stone. A handful of dry seeds is placed on a smooth stone (the metate) and ground with a mano, or handstone (a loaf-shaped rock with one flat side). The handstone is held in the hands and rubbed back and forth on the metate with a pounding, scraping motion. It is best to work with the metate placed in the middle of a blanket to avoid losing seeds in the grinding process. Wet grinding may prove easier for some. It is accomplished by dampening the seeds until they are soft and then grinding them into a dry paste (Fig. 68).

Fig. 68. Using a metate to grind seeds.

Fig. 67. Winnowing seeds by handfuls.

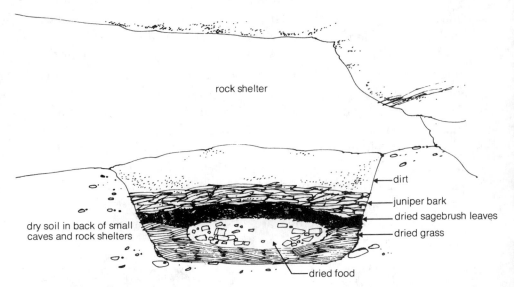

Fig. 69. Storage pit for food.

Seeds may also be dried or parched for preservation. The parching process is not difficult but requires a steady hand and a good parching tray. A tray can be made from willows woven closely to form a large, shallow bowl. A metal dishpan will also do. The bottom of the tray is covered with seeds and then a layer of hot hardwood coals is poured into it. The contents are stirred and the tray is shaken until all of the seeds are toasted. The hot coals are then flipped away and the contents of the tray are poured onto a flat rock or into a pan and cleaned by hand.

Dried seeds, roots, and berries can be safely stored in pits at the back of dry rock shelters and in crevices. A pit approximately two feet deep and lined with grass is sufficient. The dried food is placed in the pit and covered with dry sagebrush leaves and juniper bark, and then at least six inches of dirt is piled over all this (Fig. 69). A pit made in dry dust and soil beneath an overhanging ledge will remain dry for years, and insects and rodents will rarely bother it.

Barks and Greens

Barks, leaves, and stems should be stripped and picked with care, and only the young, tender portions should be selected. If possible, one should keep them fresh and cool while gathering, by placing them in

Fig. 70. Monocline slope.

the shade, covering them with a damp cloth or damp grass, or standing them in a container with a little water in it, but they must not be soaked in water to be kept fresh.

Geography of Plant Life

A knowledge of plant zones will help in the search for useful and edible species. Many useful varieties are found nearly everywhere that the elevation and latitude are right, so one can apply these principles to nearly every temperate-to-arid region on the earth.

Topography determines the flora primarily through its effect on precipitation and temperature. Altitude is more important in this respect than latitude. Generally, precipitation increases rapidly with altitude in semiarid desert or plateau regions. This affects the amount and variety of plant growth in an area and will determine what to look for in the quest for food and tools.

Mountain structure also helps determine the water runoff patterns that affect plant life. A range that is a balanced anticline has equal runoff on all sides. Most ranges, however, are monocline, with one steep escarpment and one gradual plane or dip (Fig. 70). On the steep side of the mountain, the drainage area is small and the moisture flows down the steep rocky face, much of it sinking under the thick alluvial deposits forming valley floors. The water seldom emerges as springs.

The long axial side of a mountain range has more settled deposits and more land surface to collect and channel water. Springs, creeks, and damp areas are more frequent, favoring some species of plants, while the more arid steep sides of the mountains favor other types of plants.

Also, the slopes of hills facing in a direction that catches more direct sunlight will be more arid, while the opposite side of the hill, where the sun's rays strike at a shallower angle to the land surface, will have less evaporation. The snow stays longer on that side of the hill, and evergreens, shrubs, and larger species will thrive there.

Within a given area, one may be able to walk through several "life zones" in a day or perhaps several days. Each of these life zones contributes to human existence in a very different way and consequently predetermines to a large degree the movements of an informed survivor. The flora is most important. Also, the distribution of food animals depends somewhat upon the flora.

Zones of flora correlate primarily with altitude, secondarily with latitude. The zones listed below have been named and defined in such a way as to be applicable to a broad range of the earth's temperate arid zones.

Arctic-Alpine Zone

Above timberline, usually about eleven thousand feet in altitude. In this environment the flora is restricted and scrubby and consists mainly of grasses. These are unimportant as human food sources except as they support animal species that humans can hunt, although some of the grass seeds are edible in season. Firewood is scarce, and materials for constructing tools and implements are scarce because any wood found in this zone tends to be short and twisted. A survivor would quickly leave this area for a lower elevation if at all possible.

Canadian Zone, spruce-fir belt

Nine to eleven thousand feet. The trees include some species of fir, spruce, pine, and several willows.

About sixteen species of herbaceous grasses are found here, most of which have seeds that will serve as food. The grasses may include wheat grass, redtop, bluegrass, and needlegrass.

This belt supports about twenty other characteristic plants, of which only three are considered important food plants: gooseberry, wax currant, and elderberry. Other plant species can be used for greens and root foods, but these are scarce. Plants useful for constructing tools and shelter are few and tend to be brittle. About the only wood in this belt suitable for fire-making tools is the willow, which at this altitude is considered a poor firestick.

Canadian Zone, aspen-fir belt

Seven to nine thousand feet. Trees include other species of fir, aspen, pine, and willow.

There is a great increase of edible grasses, greens, roots, and berries at this altitude. Some of them are strawberry, waterleaf, Indian potato, arrowleaf balsamroot, grasses, bracken fern, chokecherry, currant, elderberry, goldenrod, miner's lettuce, mints, mountain dandelion, mule's ears, mullein, nettles, onions, Oregon grape, plantain, raspberry, rose, salsify, sego lily, serviceberry, dock, spring beauty, thistle, violet, wild hyacinth, yampa, yarrow, and yellow fritillary.

The number of plants useful for construction increases also, with the addition of sagebrush ranging up from lower elevations, and several fiber-producing plants. Many woods useful for weapons, traps, and camp gear are available. This is still a difficult zone in which to survive indefinitely even under normal conditions, and one would be better off to move to a lower, transitional zone.

Transitional Zone, mahogany or yellow pine belt

This intermediate zone is characterized by the blending of species from the zones above it with those of the zones below it, along with its own characteristic plants. This feature alone makes survival here superior. The characteristic trees are yellow pine and scrub mahogany. Some oak brush is present.

Nearly all the edible plants listed in the aspen-fir belt are found here, as well as those found in the upper reaches of the piñon-juniper belt.

Resources for constructing shelter, fire, and tools are abundant and the weather is less severe in either extreme than in higher zones.

Upper Sonoran Zone, piñon-juniper or artemisia belt

Five to seven thousand feet. This zone occupies the greater part of most mountain ranges, foothills, and high valleys. Trees are piñon, juniper or cedar, cottonwoods, and many shrubs.

There are fewer species of edible plants, but in general the increase in volume of a single species more than compensates. Biscuit-root, sego lily, camas, cattail, and other edibles are abundant, prolific, and bulky, making harvesting easier. Chokecherry and currant berries ripen early. Many greens are present along watercourses. Notable species include amaranth, arrowhead, beeplant, grasses, bulrush, burdock, burreed, ground cherry, heron's bill, horsetail, Indian ricegrass, lamb's quarter, mallow, mints, Mormon tea, mustard, plantain, prickly pear cactus, prickly lettuce, purslane, red clover, salsify, samphire, sorrel dock, sour dock, sunflower, thistle, and watercress.

Plants for construction include serviceberry, reed, rose, sagebrush, greasewood, white willow, juniper, nettle, milkweed, dogbane, and sumac.

Aboriginal inhabitants spent most of their time in the Transitional and Upper Sonoran zones, ranging upward only seasonally for special food sources. North of the forty-second parallel, roots, tubers, and berries increase dramatically. In those areas, increased precipitation at lower altitudes produces "prairies" that abound in food plants such as camas and bitterroot.

Lower Sonoran Zone, creosote-bush or covillea belt

This zone is comprised of warm, low valleys mainly south of the thirty-seventh parallel. Here, in addition to plant forms found in other Sonoran belts, there are larger numbers of yucca and cactus species. The dominant edible plants include mesquite, screw bean, yucca, cactus, creosote bush, and Mormon tea.

This is a more important food belt than the Arctic-Alpine Zone at the other end of the scale. Survivors depend more on streams and oases for travel routes and usually find sufficient food sources along the waterways that range down from the higher belts.

Edible Plants

The following list contains many of the more important food plants found in the Great Basin plateau of the western United States. Many of these plants are pictured in the colorplate section at the end of this book.

In the rugged Great Basin region, plant life is rather restricted and in most cases adapted to arid conditions. The higher elevations produce a wider variety of edible species, which also grow in desert valleys along stream courses. Edible seeds are the most common food source and comprise over half the available species. I have supplied locations for only those plants that grow in limited habitats. I do not differentiate between native and introduced plants—if a plant grows in uncultivated areas, for our purposes here it is considered wild.

In the following list, the common name(s) is listed first, followed by the scientific—generic and species—name(s). Whenever the generic name (always capitalized and italicized) appears alone, usually many— and in some cases all—species of that genera are edible, but are too numerous to list. Whenever the species name (italicized but not capitalized) is listed after the generic name, only that species of the plant is to be used. Each color photograph shown for a given plant is of only one species, but is usually one of the most common species of the given genera and often representative of it.

Note: Some edible plants are poisonous unless prepared with caution; others are easily confused with poisonous plants. To aid the reader and to caution him, a † precedes each of these plants, both in the list given here and in the colorplate section at the end of the book.

Amaranth, Pigweed; *Amaranthus*

Description: Amaranth, an annual herb, has veiny alternate leaves and bears black seeds that grow in terminal or axillary clusters (colorplate 1).

Preparation and Uses: Pigweed is known as America's forgotten cereal grain. Its shiny black seeds make a suitable cereal raw or cooked and may be added to soups, stews, and breads. The young leaves make a superior green when cooked like spinach soon after they are picked.

In late summer the seeds may be stripped from the stalk by hand or the whole plant can be pulled up. The seeds can be threshed by beating bundles of the stalks with a stick and winnowing the chaff by tossing the seeds in a blanket. The yield may amount to a pound or more of seeds from only a small armload of plants.

Arrowhead, Wappato; *Sagittaria latifolia*

Description: Arrowhead grows in water or marshes and is easily identified by its deep green arrowhead-shaped leaves that protrude from the water or lie flat like a lily pad. The stalk is a single stem that bears fruits on lateral spikes. The fruits are round heads containing flat seeds. The fibrous root system spreads directly from the tuft of leaves and grows some distance into the shallow mud. In late fall, small tubers form on the rootstalks (colorplate 1).

Preparation and Uses: The small tubers, forming only in the late fall, can be gathered throughout the fall, winter, and early spring. One can harvest them by wading into the water and feeling in the mud with toes or hands. Large amounts can be harvested by raking the water and mud to a depth of about six inches with a forked stick. This breaks the tubers from the roots so they float to the surface. The only disadvantage to gathering arrowhead is that the weather is usually icy cold during the harvesting season and bare feet and arms suffer. In addition, one must be aware that an onslaught on streams or marshes may deplete supplies of arrowhead and thereby have a negative effect on the environment.

The tubers are roasted or baked to remove the stinging, poisonous properties. They taste something like potatoes, and can be baked, mashed into cakes, and dried for future use.

Arrowleaf Balsamroot, Balsamroot; *Balsamorrhiza*

Description: A member of the composite family, arrowleaf balsamroot is low growing and has arrow-shaped basal leaves and stems topped with yellow flowers that resemble sunflowers (colorplate 1).

Preparation and Uses: The large young root is edible when cooked. Some roots can be eaten raw but are bitter. The best way to prepare the root is to pit-steam large quantities for twenty-four hours or more and then mash and shape them into cakes for storage.

Asparagus; *Asparagus officinalis*

Description: Asparagus grows in moist ground near civilization. Its young shoots rise from the ground in early spring and later become tall and branching, bearing red berries (colorplate 2).

Preparation and Uses: The young shoots can be eaten raw or cooked and prepared like domestic asparagus.

Beeplant; *Cleome*

Description: Beeplants are annual herbs with stems that are one to three feet tall. The leaves are branching with three leaflets, and the seedpods are one to two inches in length. The flowers are yellow or rose-purple, depending on the species. These plants grow mostly in sandy ground at lower elevations (colorplate 2).

Preparation and Uses: The greens can be eaten if they are boiled in two or three changes of water to remove the bitter taste. However, they are tastier when mixed with other foods after they are cooked. The cooked shoots can be dried and used as an emergency food. After the plant is cooked for several hours, the liquid can serve as a black dye.

†Biscuit-root; Kouse; *Cymopterus*

Description: A member of the carrot family, biscuit-root consists of several edible species having swollen, bulblike roots. The plants grow in rocky places and on hillsides throughout the West and are often found in quite arid places. The flowers are borne on compound umbels and the leaves are divided into narrow segments like carrot leaves. Care should be taken not to confuse biscuit-root with related species that usually grow in damp areas and are often poisonous. Some members of the genera, such as the poison hemlock, are deadly. This family must be studied carefully for identification of the edible species (colorplate 3).

Preparation and Uses: The seeds of some species are edible when ground into mush or flour. The root is a favored ingredient of stews and tastes something like dumplings. It can be boiled or roasted in a pit for best results, and if mashed and dried in cakes after it is cooked, it will keep indefinitely. This was the famous "bread of cows" (kouse) so eagerly sought by the Lewis and Clark expedition.

Blazing Star; Stickleaf; *Mentzelia*

Description: Blazing star is a coarse, branching plant one to three feet tall, bearing beautiful yellow flowers and leaves covered with barbed hairs. Because of the barbed hairs, the lance-shaped leaves often stick to clothing. The edges of the leaves are deeply cleft, or pinnate. The root is buried deep as opposed to spreading, as in the root systems of many similar-looking plants. Blazing star sometimes grows in seleniferous soils (colorplate 3).

Preparation and Uses: The seeds, after they are parched and ground into flour or meal, can be cooked as a serviceable but not too tasty mush or bread.

Bluegrass; *Poa* (western)

Description: A grass common to rangeland, bluegrass bears seeds in narrow, spreading seed heads. It is not crucial to distinguish between the various grasses, as most that bear harvestable seeds in a grainlike husk are edible (colorplate 3).

Preparation and Uses: The seeds, if harvested with a seed beater, can be a good source of food when the season is right. But since most grass seeds drop shortly after maturity, the season is limited. Seeds may be prepared as any grain for soups, cereal, or bread.

†Bracken Fern; *Pteridium aquilinum*

Description: The most common of our ferns, bracken fern is coarse and covered with felty hairs at the base, and its young shoots uncurl in juicy stalks called fiddleheads (because of the resemblance in shape to the fiddle). The mature plant has a three-forked stem bearing light green fronds (colorplate 4).

Preparation and Uses: Young fiddleheads have long been a popular potherb in many countries. They are best when cooked like asparagus or when eaten raw with other foods. The mature fern is tough and un-palatable and may be toxic if eaten in large quantities. Under ordinary conditions, one should not uproot the plant for food. Some people are sensitive to the mature leaves.

Bristlegrass, Foxtail Millet: *Seteria*

Description: A grass with dense foxtail-like seed spikes having long, stiff bristles, bristlegrass is a common species of wasteland and desert seeps (colorplate 4).

Preparation and Uses: The grain of this plant is similar to that of wheat or millet and is easily obtained by parching to remove the husks. The seeds, ground for flour or boiled for cereal, provide excellent nourish-ment.

Buffaloberry; *Shepherdia argentea, S. canadensis*

Description: A shrub or small tree, buffaloberry is somewhat thorny with oval or nearly oval leaves. Its small red berries last late into the fall.

Preparation and Uses: The berries are edible and can be cooked in stews or dried and pounded for meal and pemmican. The taste of the sum-mer berries may be strange to some palates, but they are not poisonous, as many people have assumed.

Bulrush; *Scirpus*

Description: Bulrush often grows taller than a man and has stems that are triangular in some species and round in others. A cluster of sets grows at or near the tip. Bulrush grows along streams and in marshes (colorplate 5).

Preparation and Uses: The rootstalks are edible and should be peeled and boiled or eaten raw. The center core of the root is especially tasty. The young shoots just protruding from the mud are a delicacy raw or cooked. One harvests them by wading into the water and feeling down along the plant until he comes to the last shoot in a string of shoots that protrude above the water. He pushes his hands into the mud until he finds the lateral rootstalk. By feeling along the rootstalk in a direction away from the last shoot, one can often find a protruding bulb from which the new shoot is starting. This is easily snapped off and can be eaten on the spot. When the only available water is brackish, these young shoots will allay thirst for a long time.

The rootstalks, when peeled, dried, and pounded into flour, make a good bread. This flour can be mixed with a flour made from the seeds of the same plant. These are harvested by stripping and winnowing and are an important source of grain food.

The slender stalks are generally too tough for eating, but they are useful as cordage or for sandals, baskets, and mats.

Burdock; *Arctium minus*

Description: Every farmer knows this bothersome weed. Burdock is characterized by large rhubarblike leaves and purple flowers that produce a soft burr. The leaves are often over ten inches wide and a foot long and are smooth and velvety to the touch. The burrs are characterized by a mass of slender hooked spines that are not stiff. They cling to clothes and socks but seldom prick the skin (colorplates 5, 6).

Preparation and Uses: This useful plant has long been used in folk medicine for various external and internal complaints, generally as a tonic. The young leaves and shoots are edible when cooked as greens, and the root of the first-year plant is an excellent food when fried or roasted. If boiled, the root may be tough and strong-tasting unless the water is changed at least once.

The young stalks of the burdock can be peeled of their tough, bitter rind and the pithy centers boiled for food. The roots can be dried and stored.

Burreed; *Sparganium*

Description: Aquatic plants with branching, leafy stems, burreeds have small round seed heads resembling burrs, located on the sides and near the top of the stalks (colorplate 6).

Preparation and Uses: The bulbous stems and tuberous roots of this plant are used for food in much the same way as cattails and bulrushes.

†Camas; *Camassia*

Description: Camas, a member of the lily family growing in damp meadows, is characterized by grasslike, slender leaves radiating from the base. The stem is usually one or two feet tall and topped with a spike of blue flowers (colorplates 6, 7). It should never be confused with the similar-looking death camas or *Zigadenus*, which is easily distinguished by its smaller, yellow or cream-colored flowers (colorplate 7). Careless identification has caused the deaths of many wild-plant eaters, as death camas is extremely poisonous. Nor should the common name, camas, be used as a guide to edibility, because an altogether different plant, *Veratrum*, is also called camas and should be considered poisonous.

Camas should be harvested only when the plant is in bloom, for it is at this time that the survivalist can most easily distinguish it from the white death camas. It can be harvested at other times of year only by those who are very familiar with the plant's minute characteristics. It is possible, after much observing of both plants, to distinguish between them, both before and after flowering. Camas is never found growing in dry, rocky ground, as is the death camas; the leaf blades of most camas are slightly broader than those of most species of death camas; generally the bulbs of large, mature camas are much larger than the largest bulbs of the death camas; camas grows mostly in the northern areas of the West: Idaho, Oregon, and Washington.

Preparation and Uses: The starchy bulb is an excellent food and can be gathered in large quantities with a digging stick. In meadows where these plants grow, a bushel can be gathered in a few hours. The bulbs are best prepared by baking in a pit oven. After they are cooked, they can be mashed and dried in cakes for storage. Camas bulbs were an important source of food to many early Native American tribes.

Cattail; *Typha*

Description: Found along streams and marshes throughout the West, cattail has bladelike leaves as much as six feet long and a jointless stem terminating in a sausage-shaped seed head (colorplate 7).

Preparation and Uses: The cattail is an outstanding edible plant. The roots, young shoots, seed heads, and pollen are all edible, and the leaves make an excellent material for weaving. The down from the head makes a good insulation for blankets and sleeping bags.

The roots, when peeled and dried, can be made into flour for bread. One can also obtain the starch from the roots by mashing and soaking them in water and stirring the mixture vigorously. After they have been stirred, the roots should be removed and the water allowed to sit overnight or until all the starch settles to the bottom of the container. The water is then poured off and the starch used as dough for making bread.

The young shoots are excellent when eaten raw or boiled like asparagus. The centers of the older shoots can be eaten the same way but are not as good.

In the early summer the spikes at the top of the seed head form clusters of yellow-colored pollen, which is very light and fine. It can be stripped from the stalks with the fingers and put into tight containers or bags to be used as flour for bread. It is epecially good when mixed with coarser flour made from grain.

Before the pollen appears, the green heads can be boiled and eaten like corn on the cob. When dry, the heads can be burned, leaving only the tiny roasted seeds, which can be eaten as mush or ground for flour. A large quantity of cattail heads yields only a small quantity of seeds.

The down, stuffed between two blankets that have been sewn together, will give excellent insulation in cold weather; stuffed into shoes, it will help prevent frostbite.

The leaves, stripped and dried, can be used to make matting and other woven materials like sandals, baskets, blankets, and ponchos.

Chicory; *Cichorium intybus*

Description: Chicory leaves resemble the leaves of a dandelion, but the chicory stem is branching and stiff. In late summer, blue flowers appear on the stiff, irregular stalks.

Preparation and Uses: The leaves are used as a potherb much as dandelions are, and the roots are edible in emergencies.

Chokecherry; *Prunus virginiana*

Description: Chokecherry, a tree or shrub, is easily recognized in the fall by its clusters of red-black cherries. The bark is reddish grey and somewhat speckled with lateral lines that resemble those on the bark of the domestic cherry tree (colorplate 8).

Preparation and Uses: The cherries of this tree are an excellent food despite the cyanogenetic poison contained in the seed. The cherries without the pits are puckery but good raw. Cooked, they make an excellent jam. Slightly dried and crushed — seeds and all — in a mortar and dried in cakes, these berries provide nourishment that is lasting and satisfying. Before they are eaten, the cakes must be cooked to neutralize the poison in the seeds. Pemmican is made by mixing fat and pounded dried meat with the meal of chokecherries and sealing it in gut or molding it into round balls for preservation.

Cottonwood; *Populus*

Description: Large trees growing along streams at most elevations, the cottonwoods have rough grey bark and bear flowers in drooping catkins that are borne in broad disks. The buds of these trees are resinous, and the leaves are serrated, with long petioles (colorplate 8).

Preparation and Uses: The buds and leaves often provide an edible honeydew made by aphids. It is scraped from the leaves or skimmed off the surface of the water in which the leaves have been boiled. The inner bark and the sap of the tree are also useful emergency foods.

Currant; *Ribes*

Description: A shrub three to ten feet tall, the currant has toothed leaves and berries forming in clusters. The berries are gold, red, or black (colorplate 9).

Preparation and Uses: The berries ripen early and provide an excellent food that can be eaten fresh or dried. They may be prepared in any of the ways mentioned for chokecherries. None are known to contain poisons, and they can be used or eaten in large quantities. The stems of the currant make excellent arrowshafts.

†Elderberry; *Sambucus*

Description: Elderberry, a large shrub, is characterized by a large, pithy, brown-colored stem bearing opposite compound leaves. The berries grow in flat-topped clusters and are deep purple when ripe (colorplate 9).

Preparation and Uses: The berries ripen in fall, when they become an important food source. They can be eaten raw or cooked. They keep well when dried and tend to lose their rank flavor. The flower clusters may be eaten dipped in a batter and fried or crushed into stew. The green leaves and stems of the plant are said to be poisonous. The pith of this plant is poisonous. The stems make excellent bow and hand drills for firemaking.

Evening Primrose; *Oenothera*

Description: Two species of evening primrose can be found in the arid West. The low-growing species appears coarse, with long leaves growing from the crown of the root and large white flowers. The taller species is rather stiff and erect, somewhat prickly and coarse, with yellow flowers. The flowers of all the plants remain open during the night (colorplate 10).

Preparation and Uses: The seeds of various species can be eaten parched or ground into meal. Many of the species have bitter roots that are not very palatable, but some lose this property when dug in early spring and cooked. When made palatable, the roots are an important source of food in foothills and mountains.

Goldenrod; *Solidago*

Description: A tall plant with a long inflorescence crowded in a cluster and leaves that are often toothed, hairy, and alternate on the stem (colorplate 10).

Preparation and Uses: The seeds are used as a thickening for stews. The young leaves and flowers make a potherb and tea.

Greasewood; *Sarcobatus*

Description: A stiff, light-colored bush with spring shoots forming some-times straight clusters of growth, greasewood grows in alkaline soils, usually near water sources (colorplate 10).

Preparation and Uses: The new spring tops are an edible source of salt. The wood is very hard, good for digging sticks, arrow foreshafts, trap triggers, and a variety of tools requiring a sharp point.

Ground Cherry, Husk Tomato; *Physalis*

Description: A low, trailing plant, ground cherry bears yellow flowers that later form husks or bladders containing a small fruit that resembles a tomato. The leaves are usually oblong and bluntly pointed (colorplate 11).

Preparation and Uses: The fruit may be eaten raw or baked into ashcakes, cooked in stews, or made into jam.

Groundsel; *Senecio*

Description: Usually found in moist or wet meadows. The leaves are lance shaped and dissected into narrow divisions, and its flowers are yellow. The plant is covered with tiny hairs that impart a grey sheen. The plant contains a sticky sap (colorplate 11).

Preparation and Uses: The young leaves are edible as a potherb. They are also used to line cooking pits.

Hairgrass; *Deschampsia*

Description: A fine-textured grass of higher altitudes, it is found in wet or damp soils (colorplate 11).

Preparation and Uses: The seeds may be harvested with a seed beater and ground for mush and flour.

Heron's Bill, Storkbill; *Erodium cicutarium*

Description: An herb that may form rosettes and later have spreading stems, heron's bill bears rose to lavender flowers. The seed resembles a stork's bill. These plants grow in open dry ground throughout the West (colorplate 12).

Preparation and Uses: The young plants are cooked for greens or eaten raw as salad.

Horsetail, Scouring Rush, Jointgrass, Snakegrass: *Equisetum*

Description: Horsetail is the common jointgrass so eagerly sought after by children for playthings. The stems are of two kinds: one is sterile and has many branches; the other is fertile and has no branches. The grass is jointed and pulls apart easily, and at the top of each fertile stem is a brown head (colorplate 12).

Preparation and Uses: The young shoots in spring can be used as a potherb. Later the shoots become too stiff and contain a silica that gives them the name "scouring rush." They can then be used for cleaning metal, for polishing and honing bone implements and wooden shafts, and for sharpening pocketknives.

Indian Potato; *Orogenia linearifolia*

Description: Indian potato is a tiny plant with basal leaves that are divided into slender leaflets that look like bird tracks. The stem arises from a deep nutlike bulb, and the tiny white flowers grow in compound umbels (colorplate 13).

Preparation and Uses: This was a favorite of the Native Americans. The bulb can be boiled, steamed, roasted, or baked in any of the ways used for potatoes. The tiny bulbs are also tasty when eaten raw. They may be cooked and mashed into cakes for drying. They keep indefinitely when protected from moisture. The hard cakes can then be soaked and cooked in stews or soups. One of the tastiest roots found in the West, this plant grows in meadows and on mountainsides at higher altitudes.

†Indian Ricegrass; *Oryzopsis hymenoides*

Description: Indian ricegrass has slender stems and flat or in-rolled leaves and a tufted seed head that contains large grains. This plant is found on sand dunes and in desert areas (colorplate 13).

Preparation and Uses: The seeds are ground for cereal. This grain is abundant and easily harvested. Seed heads containing black seeds should be discarded, as they may harbor a harmful fungus infection.

Jerusalem Artichoke, Sunflower; *Helianthus tuberosus*

Description: A species of sunflower introduced from the Midwest and found growing in waste areas, jerusalem artichoke is usually more slender than the native sunflower of the West. It has large potatolike roots in the fall (colorplate 14).

Preparation and Uses: The large tuber is edible and formed an important food for the Native Americans of the Midwest. It has largely escaped cultivation in the West and is not generally found in unsettled areas.

Juniper, Cedar; *Juniperus*

Description: Evergreen shrubs or trees with blue berries, junipers are very common in the foothills and desert portions of the West (colorplates 14, 15).

Preparation and Uses: The blue juniper berries are bitter but nutritious and can be eaten in an emergency. If they are pounded and boiled, some of the bitter taste is removed. The inner white bark, stripped and pounded into a meal, will hold off starvation for a time.

Lamb's Quarter, Goosefoot; *Chenopodium*

Description: Lamb's quarter is a common weed of wastelands and stream banks. The leaves vary from ovate to lanceolate in the various species, and the seeds form in clusters (colorplate 15).

Preparation and Uses: The leaves and stems are edible when young. They can be eaten as salad or cooked like spinach. The seeds are also edible; they are ground into flour and baked into bread when mixed with other grain flour.

Mallow, Cheeseweed; *Malva*

Description: Annual plants with thick roots and stems that run along the ground, mallows bear small white to pale blue flowers. The fruit is round and flattened into the shape of a cheese wheel, hence the name "cheesies." These plants are found around cultivated areas (colorplate 15).

Preparation and Uses: Mallows can be used as a potherb, and the leaves and stems may be cooked in soups. The fruit is excellent eaten raw or cooked, and the dried leaves make a superior warm drink.

Mannagrass; *Glyceria*

Description: Mannagrass has long narrow leaves and a long seed head. It is often found growing on stream banks and around seeps, and its long leaves sometimes hang into the water and float.

Preparation and Uses: The seeds are gathered with a seed beater, winnowed to remove the chaff, and used as a thickening for soups and stews. They can be ground on a metate for flour. Mannagrass is one of the better-tasting grains found growing in the West.

Maple, Box Elder; *Acer negundo*

Description: A tree with leaves composed of three to five separate leaflets and winged seeds, the box elder is common to mountain valleys and gullies (colorplate 16).

Preparation and Uses: The winged seeds are roasted and eaten. Pounded for flour, the inner bark serves as an emergency food. When sap rises in late winter, the sweet sap can be boiled down into a good maple syrup.

†Milkweed; *Asclepias syriaca*

Description: The stout stems of milkweed bear opposite entire leaves with broad midribs, and when broken, the stems and leaves emit a milky sap. The large pods, formed after flowering, bear seeds that are plumed with silky fibers (colorplate 16).

Preparation and Uses: Some milkweeds are highly poisonous. However, if a person carefully distinguishes *Asclepias syriaca* from the deadly dog-bane, which is similar in appearance, the young shoots of milkweed can be cooked and eaten. The very young seedpods can be boiled and eaten, also. The sap may be heated for chewing gum and the stalk fibers used to make cordage and fishline.

Miner's Lettuce, Indian Lettuce; *Montia*

Description: Indian lettuce is a small, succulent plant with round, fleshy leaves. Some of the leaves are joined to each other on both sides in such a way as to form a rounded disk or cup (colorplate 16).

Preparation and Uses: This tasty plant is the rival of garden lettuce for salads and raw greens and can be eaten in large quantities. When mixed with watercress and placed between two hotcakes of Indian potato root dough, it is unexcelled for flavor and constitutes a rare and satisfying sandwich.

Mint; *Mentha* and other genera

Description: Members of the mint family are characterized by a square stem and opposite leaves (colorplate 17).

Preparation and Uses: Catnip, peppermint, horehound, spearmint, sage, thyme, hyssop, and several other plants of the mint family are used for food and drink. As drinks, some are unmatched for their soothing qualities and often relieve headache, nausea, colic, and other nervous upsets that may be encountered in the wilds. The seeds can be eaten or added to the leaves for steeping.

Mormon Tea, Brigham Tea, Squaw Tea; *Ephedra*

Description: A shrub with stiff green jointed branches and scale-like leaves, Mormon tea is found in the southern portions of the West and is easily identified (colorplate 18).

Preparation and Uses: The green stems can be steeped for a soothing drink, but the beverage may stain the teeth if used regularly.

Mountain Dandelion, False Dandelion; *Agoseris*

Description: Mountain dandelion looks like the common dandelion with its yellow flower; however, its leaves may or may not be toothed (colorplate 18).

Preparation and Uses: The leaves and roots are edible when cooked. The hardened sap or juice from the root and stems is also edible and can be used as chewing gum.

Mule's Ears; *Wyethia*

Description: *Wyethia amplexicaulis* has flower heads that resemble those of the sunflower. They are bright yellow or orange-yellow, and several heads grow on a stalk. The plant itself grows low to the ground, and its leaves are erect and glossy. *Wyethia helianthoides* is similar in appearance, having white flowers and a sticky, hairy stalk. These two species of mule's ears often crossbreed and produce hybrids that bear yellow flowers on hairy stalks (colorplate 18).

Preparation and Uses: The seeds are edible, and the roots of *Wyethia helianthoides* can be eaten after they are cooked for at least thirty hours in a steaming-pit. Even then some people have to hold their noses to get it down.

Mustard, Shepherd's Purse, White Top, Peppergrass; *Sisymbrium, Brassica, Lepidium,* and other genera

Description: These common mustards of every barnyard and wasteland are evident in several forms. They are generally a leafy weed, erect with yellow or white flowers. The leaves are often deeply cleft (colorplates 19, 20).

Preparation and Uses: The seeds of all the species are edible, as well as the young greens, which are eaten as a potherb.

Nettle, Stinging Nettle; *Urtica*

Description: Nettle is an erect plant with opposite toothed leaves that are long and pointed at the outer end. The stalks, stems, and leaves are covered with fine stinging hairs that are well known to most picnickers (colorplate 20).

Preparation and Uses: The leaves and young stems are edible as cooked greens. They are gathered with gloves or with large mullein leaves (*Verbascum*) used as pads for the hands. The stinging properties are removed by cooking. The dried stalks in fall are an excellent source of fiber for cordage.

†Oak; *Quercus*

Description: Oaks range all the way from a shrub six inches high to the small common scrub oak that grows in the mountains to the large tree that grows in fertile valleys. *Q. Gambelli* is the most important in the Great Basin (colorplate 20).

Preparation and Uses: The acorn can serve as an emergency food but must be leached of its tannic acid before it is eaten. The wood is used for digging sticks and bows.

Onion, Wild Garlic, Nodding Onion; *Allium*

Description: Resembling the domestic onions, these small wild onions and garlics always have the familiar onion smell when their leaves are bruised. Plants looking like onions but lacking the characteristic smell should be checked closely, as some species such as death camas (*Zigadenus*) are very poisonous. Late in the season one can find the small onion plant by first finding the stalk. The dried flower head on the stalk looks like a white ball against the ground (colorplate 21).

Preparation and Uses: The whole plant is edible raw or cooked and is an excellent addition to any dish.

Oregon Grape, Algerita; *Mahonia*

Description: Oregon grape is a shrub with hollylike leaflets that grows low to the ground in dense thickets and under trees. Its leaves are spiny and dark green. In the Southwest, some species of *Mahonia* form large bushes or even trees bearing palatable fruit (colorplates 21, 22).

Preparation and Uses: The deep purple or red berries are edible raw or cooked and are rather tasty and tart. They can be dried for future use. The root makes a superior yellow dye.

Piñon Pine; *Pinus monophylla, P. edulis*

Description: An evergreen tree that grows in many areas of the West, the piñon pine is characterized by its spreading growth and dense covering of pinecones containing large seeds (colorplate 22).

Preparation and Uses: The cones can be gathered and charred in a fire to roast and loosen the seeds. They then are beaten from the cones and used as one of the most important foods available in nature. They may be eaten shelled or ground, shell and all, on a metate.

Plantain; *Plantago major, P. lanceolata*

Description: Plantain, a common lawn pest, grows in two varieties. *Plantago major* has flat leaves and *Plantago lanceolata* has long, lance-shaped leaves, both dark green and ribbed. The seed heads grow in dense clusters at the end of long stems. The whole plant is only about eight inches tall (colorplate 22).

Preparation and Uses: The young leaves can be eaten and are an important herb for dressing wounds (see Medicinal Plants at the end of this chapter).

Prickly Lettuce, Wild Lettuce; *Lactuca*

Description: A common weed, prickly lettuce has several species, most with narrow lobed leaves. The plant bleeds a milky juice when injured (colorplate 23).

Preparation and Uses: The young leaves are edible when cooked, and the gum of the roots can be made into chewing gum.

†Prickly Pear Cactus; *Opuntia*

Description: The prickly pear cactus has pear-shaped pads and fruits, and large patches grow on hillsides and deserts throughout the West. Many other cacti are also edible but should be identified before they are eaten (colorplates 23, 24).

Preparation and Uses: The fruits and new joints of this plant should be scorched or peeled. They can then be eaten raw or cooked, and the seeds can be ground into flour. Some cacti may be over one hundred years old; care should be taken not to destroy them.

Purslane; *Portulaca oleracea*

Description: A small weed growing low to the ground, purslane has smooth, fleshy leaves with rounded ends and stems that are usually rose colored and juicy (colorplate 24).

Preparation and Uses: The whole plant is edible as a potherb or salad green.

†Rabbitbrush; *Chrysothamnus*

Description: Rabbitbrush, a stiff, light-colored bush with new green stems at the top, grows in alkaline soils, usually around water holes and lakes (colorplate 24).

Preparation and Uses: Rabbitbrush is poisonous to livestock. However, the secretion at the top of the roots can be chewed for gum.

Raspberry, Thimbleberry, Black Cap; *Rubus*

Description: All species are brambly shrubs, some having spines with red, black, purple, blue, or orange berries, and all belong to the rose family. The common wild raspberry is perhaps the most prevalent (colorplate 25).

Preparation and Uses: The berries are edible in season and can be dried for future use.

Red Clover; *Trifolium*

Description: Wild red clover, with its round flower head and three leaves, resembles the domestic variety (colorplate 25).

Preparation and Uses: The seeds are edible as well as the greens, and the steeped leaves and flowers are reputed to be good for colds and coughs.

Reed, Reed Canary Grass; *Phragmites communis*

Description: Long-jointed and stout with hollow stems, reeds resemble cane or bamboo (colorplate 25).

Preparation and Uses: The seeds are edible when cooked as cereal. The roots may also be eaten when cooked, and the young shoots are edible raw or cooked. The plant's main value is as a material for weaving or making arrowshafts.

Rose, Wild Rose; *Rosa*

Description: Every camper knows this thorny bush. The wild rose looks like the domestic rosebush, with reddish stems bearing bright red fruit, or hips, that mature in fall after the first frost (colorplate 26).

Preparation and Uses: Rose hips are a ready supply of nutritious food that lasts through the fall and often all winter. They are easily picked and ground on a metate for a meal or for flour, but the fresh fruit is also good when cooked. The numerous seeds are hard and must be cracked or ground before they are eaten. Rose hips contain a massive dose of vitamin C and are very nourishing. The stems of this plant make the best arrowshafts.

Salsify, Oysterplant, Goatsbeard; *Tragopogon*

Description: The leaves of salsify are grasslike and slightly hairy, giving them a queer translucent appearance around the edges. The second-year plants produce yellow or purple flowers that later form large seed heads with umbrella-like fluffs that carry the seeds away in the wind (colorplates 26, 27).

Preparation and Uses: The first-year roots are edible when cooked, but as the first-year plant produces only leaves without flowers, it is often hard to recognize. The root of the second-year plant tastes like steamed oysters and is a rich wilderness food.

Samphire; *Salicornia*

Description: Small, light green, and branching, samphire has fleshy stems reaching up like claws and is found in saline bogs and marshes (colorplate 27).

Preparation and Uses: The plant is edible raw or cooked and is a good source of salt. Added to stew, it provides all the salt flavoring necessary.

Sego Lily; *Calochortus*

Description: The small grasslike leaves of the sego lily grow among brush and trees in the foothills. Later a stem appears, bearing a lovely yellow, creamy white, or bluish flower with light purple splotches at the base of the petals. As the state flower of Utah, it should be harvested only in emergencies or for scientific purposes. At one time the plant was thought to be almost extinct; it now grows abundantly in many areas, though it is still much less widespread than formerly. Some of the plants do not bloom, which often leads the layman to believe that the species is rare (colorplate 27).

Preparation and Uses: The tender bulb, harvested with a digging stick, is unsurpassed in flavor when roasted or boiled. It can also be cooked and mashed into cakes for preservation.

Serviceberry; *Amelanchier*

Description: The serviceberries, shrubs or small trees, have simple leaves and blueberry-like fruits that resemble tiny apples when ripe (colorplate 28).

Preparation and Uses: The berries may be cooked or dried, mashed into cakes for drying, or mixed with dried meat for pemmican. The wood makes digging sticks, arrow foreshafts, and round bows.

†Sour Dock, Sorrel, Curly Dock, Yellow Dock, Wild Rhubarb, Indian Tobacco; *Rumex*

Description: The stems of sour dock are grooved, resembling rhubarb, and the flowers grow in clusters and form large seed clusters that turn brown in fall (colorplate 28).

Preparation and Uses: If chopped and then boiled for a long time into syrup, the stems are especially good. If not too bitter, they may be eaten raw like rhubarb, but the leaves may be toxic if they contain too much oxalic acid.

Spring Beauty; *Claytonia lanceolata*

Description: A tiny plant, spring beauty is found in wooded areas and grows from a round nutlike corm. Its small white or pink flowers bloom early in the spring, and its leaves grow opposite on the stem in one pair (colorplate 29).

Preparation and Uses: An important source of food in the spring, the small bulbs are dug with a digging stick and prepared in any of the ways used to prepare potatoes. They also preserve readily after they are cooked and mashed into cakes for drying.

Strawberry, Wild Strawberry; *Fragaria americana*

Description: This strawberry is like the domestic variety, only smaller (colorplate 29).

Preparation and Uses: The berry is eaten in season and the leaves are steeped for an excellent hot drink.

Sumac, Squawbush; *Rhus trilobata*

Description: Sumac is a sprawling shrub with a three-lobed leaf or with three leaflets to a leaf that has broad outer ends; its berries form in clusters and are very sticky (colorplate 29).

Preparation and Uses: The berries serve as an emergency food and an even better drink. Steeped in water and drunk cold, they are very refreshing. The stems of the plant make the best material for weaving baskets.

Sunflower; *Helianthus*

Description: This is the common sunflower easily recognized by almost anyone. Its flower is a large yellow head and it has rather prickly, hairy stalks (colorplate 30).

Preparation and Uses: The seeds of sunflowers are perhaps the most nourishing food found in the wilds. Harvested with a seed beater and then ground on a metate, they are used as mush. They should not be cooked, but just heated or eaten cold. They also make an excellent baby food; the Native Americans relied on them to a great extent for that purpose.

Thistle; *Cirsium*

Description: Many species of thistle exist, but generally they all may be described as succulent plants with many spines on the leaves and stems (colorplate 30).

Preparation and Uses: The young tender plant stems can be peeled and eaten, and their first-year roots are good when boiled with other food.

Thornapple, Haw, Hawthorn; *Crataegus*

Description: Thornapple is the only native American tree with large thorns. It looks somewhat like an apple tree, and its fruits resemble miniature crabapples.

Preparation and Uses: The berries are good food when dried and made into cakes. The dried cakes, ground and mixed with pounded jerky, make pemmican.

Umbrella Plant, Trumpet Plant, Wild Buckwheat; *Eriogonum*

Description: The leafless stalks of umbrella plant are topped by compound umbels of tiny yellow or cream-colored flowers, and the stem arises from a dense cluster of leaves that are matted on the ground. The leaves are usually lance shaped and are white on the underside. The plant grows in open areas of dry soil up to nine thousand feet in elevation (colorplate 30).

Preparation and Uses: The leaves are cooked for greens, and the seeds are edible after they are ground on a metate into meal or into flour for making bread.

Violet, Dogtooth, Glacier Lily; *Erythronium grandiflorum*

Description: In spite of its name, violet is not a violet but a lily with a yellow flower and two large shiny oblong leaves arising from the base. The petals are very recurved, and the bulb is rounded and grows deep in the soil. The plant is found at higher altitudes along streams and in shaded woodlands (colorplate 31).

Preparation and Uses: The bulb is dug with a digging stick but is difficult to obtain because it grows so deep. The bulbs are excellent when cooked like potatoes, and they can also be cooked and mashed for storage. In addition, the leaves are edible as greens. The violet is a rare plant and should be used only in emergencies.

Watercress; *Nasturtium officinale*

Description: Green and leafy and growing in clear water, watercress has white threadlike roots that form thick mats along the edges of streams. The leaves of this plant have three to nine segments. Watercress also bears tiny white flowers (colorplate 31).

Preparation and Uses: Watercress, which has a pleasant tangy taste, is a favorite salad plant used raw as greens. Watercress and miner's lettuce, wrapped together in tortillas made from root flour, make an excellent wilderness sandwich. Watercress is the host plant for liver flukes, so it should be harvested only in water that is unused by livestock.

Waterleaf; *Hydrophyllum*

Description: The delicate waterleaf grows at higher altitudes on damp hillsides among dense growth of brush and trees. Its flower is a globular head of tiny white or purple flowers, and its leaves are broad, fleshy, and deeply divided, with rounded tips (colorplate 31).

Preparation and Uses: The whole plant is edible. The rootstalks, which are several tiny brown carrotlike appendages radiating from the base of the stem, make excellent stew, and the plant tops serve as greens.

Wheat Grass, Blue Jointgrass, Quack Grass; *Agropyron*

Description: This is the common wheat grass and other similar species that are found throughout the West. It has a wheatlike seed head that contains a nutritious grain.

Preparation and Uses: The seeds are harvested with a seed beater and ground on a metate. They can be gathered in goodly amounts with a little patience. The rootstalks of this plant are also edible.

†Wild Hyacinth; *Brodiaea*

Description: Wild hyacinth has slender basal leaves and flowers—usually blue—that grow in clusters forming umbels. It is easily confused with camas or wild onion when not in bloom. Also, the name hyacinth is misleading, for domestic hyacinth is poisonous (colorplate 32).

Preparation and Uses: The bulb, an important food source in higher elevations, is best cooked and eaten with greens or mashed and dried for future use in stews. Harvesting it with a digging stick is difficult because it grows deep.

Wild Rye; *Elymus*

Description: A common bunchgrass seen along roadsides and in deserts, wild rye is coarse and tall. The plants are characterized by their flat leaves, and they bear a single erect spike of seeds at the end of each stem.

Preparation and Uses: The seeds are harvested by stripping or with a seed beater. Carefully winnowed, they make an excellent grain for mush and flour if the chaff is singed.

†Yampa, Wild Caraway; *Perideridia*

Description: A slender plant, yampa grows on damp hillsides and meadows in the foothills of the plateau area. The leaves are compound with narrow grasslike leaflets and usually dry up by flowering time. The flowers are borne in small white compound umbels. The plant is a member of the carrot family and positive identification is necessary before it is eaten. Typically, the fruit is required for positive identification.

Preparation and Uses: The small fingerlike roots grow deep and sometimes form in groups of two or three. Perhaps some of the most important and tastiest roots found, they far outrank potatoes in flavor and can be cooked in any of the ways used for potatoes. When cooked and mashed into cakes for drying, they keep a long time.

Yellow Fritillary, Yellowbell; *Fritillaria pudica*

Description: The small yellow fritillary has lanceolate basal leaves and a single yellow or golden flower that hangs either sideways or down from the bent stalk. The root is a corm with a cluster of tiny ricelike bulblets surrounding it. The plant grows among the brush on damp hillsides (colorplate 32).

Preparation and Uses: The corm is edible, as are the ricelike bulblets, and when cooked they resemble rice in both appearance and taste. The green seed heads can also be eaten after they are cooked.

Medicinal Plants

Plants are necessary not only as food but also as mild medicine. The following plants have proved most helpful to people who have suffered from minor irritations, wounds, and burns while in the wilds.

Biscuit-root, Kouse; *Cymopterus*

The old roots of biscuit-root are an effective insecticide when boiled. Sprinkle the tea around camp and in sleeping areas (colorplate 3).

Burdock; *Arctium minus*

The young roots of first-year burdock dug in early spring or late fall are often used as a salve or wash for burns, wounds, and skin irritations (colorplates 5, 6).

Cattail; *Typha*

The white starchy roots of the cattail have been pounded and mixed with animal fat and used as a salve for dressing burns (colorplate 7).

Chokecherry; *Prunus virginiana*

The inner bark of chokecherry has sometimes been used to brew a tea to check diarrhea (colorplate 8).

Mullein; *Verbascum thapsus*

The burned leaves of mullein, used as an incense, have been helpful in relieving lung congestion (colorplate 19).

Nettle, Stinging Nettle; *Urtica*

The root and leaves of nettle, when brewed into a tea, will stop diarrhea, but overuse can cause constipation (colorplate 20).

Onion, Wild Garlic, Nodding Onion; *Allium*

The mashed leaves of wild onion rubbed on the arms and neck are an effective insect repellent. However, because of their odor, they are also a very effective people repellent (colorplate 21).

Peppermint; *Mentha piperita*

Peppermint is an aromatic stimulant and has been used to relieve nausea, colic, nervous headache, and heartburn.

Pines; *Pinus*

The pitch of the lodgepole pine has been used for disinfecting and protecting open sores. The young shoots of the western white pine are boiled and used as cough syrup or as a mild drink for treating coughs and upset stomachs.

Plantain; *Plantago*

The fresh leaves of plantain act as a mild astringent when mashed to a pulp and applied to cuts and other wounds (colorplate 22).

Rose, Wild Rose; *Rosa*

Very rich in vitamins A and C, wild rose hips are eaten raw or crushed and used to brew a tea (colorplate 26).

Serviceberry; *Amelanchier*

The boiled green inner bark of serviceberry has been used for an eyewash (colorplate 28).

Sour Dock; *Rumex crispus*

The roots of curly dock can be crushed and used as a poultice on sores and swellings (colorplate 28).

Sweet Flag; *Acorus calamus*

The root of sweet flag, when steeped and drunk as a tea, has been used to relieve upset stomach.

Yarrow; *Achillea millefolium*

The leaves of yarrow are often used to stop bleeding in wounds, to reduce inflammation, and to heal rashes when applied directly to the wounded area. They are also used for tea and for relief of toothache when chewed (colorplate 32).

Directions for Gathering Botanicals

- Leaves of biennials are most valuable during their second year of growth. Leaves should always be collected in clear dry weather in the morning after the dew is off, and are at their best when the plant is in bloom.

- Flowers are worth more medicinally if used as soon as they open.

- Bulbs and roots are most useful if gathered at the time the leaves of the plant die back in the autumn.

- Only the inner bark, preferably gathered in the fall, should be used.

Fig. 71. Hunting and killing—justified only by sincere need.

Animals

Paiute Deadfall Discovery

Secret treasures lie hidden in the most unlikely places—in the spiny nests of pack rats or packed closely and tightly in the backs of crevices along cliffs. Many are centuries old, the repositories of debris dating from aboriginal times. It has been my practice to poke around in these places looking for bits of history and a story or two.

In a tiny crevice at the back of a small cave on Salmon Falls Creek, near my home, one day I plucked from a pile of sticks and cactus spines an ancient Paiute stick carefully carved with a stone knife. On one end was tied a piece of string made from the fibers of the dogbane plant. At the end of the string was a small stick inserted between the two-ply fiber and held tightly by its natural twist. For me it was a great find. I carefully took the well-preserved object and placed it in a quart jar, where it sat on my desk for many months. I looked at it and contemplated its use in the life of the person who made it. I thought it must be part of a deadfall trap of some kind, but for the life of me I could not figure out what. Finally, in order to determine its use, I made a replica of it and began experimenting. It was a frustrating experience to try to create a deadfall when I knew there were missing parts. I cut every length and size of stick I could think of and added them to my deadfall in order to create a trigger mechanism that worked. Instead I just got bruised fingers when the rock would awkwardly fall from my crude device.

Then one day it happened. It took place in my head to begin with and just naturally flowed out to my fingertips as I whittled a new stick, and it dawned on me that this apparatus was not the trigger, but the support for the trigger. I had read in Julian Steward's book, *Basin-Plateau Aboriginal Socio-Political Groups*, that the Paiutes were ingenious in the number of traps they had invented and that some of them were so efficient that they could hold up a ten-pound rock with only a tiny grass stem. Once that memory settled into me, it only took a few moments to figure it out. I had, by myself, reinvented the finest hair-trigger deadfall known to man. I named it the Paiute deadfall. It was far more sensitive than the standard figure-4 deadfall I had been using, and my trapline catch multiplied accordingly.

A few years later I was able to confirm the accuracy of this reinvention when Margaret Wheat published her book, *Survival Arts of the Primitive Paiutes*, showing photographs of an old Nevada Paiute man demonstrating a similar device whose construction had been taught to him by his grandfather. It was a thrilling moment. Such a small thing made all the difference in the simple process of living off the land.

Animal life is an important and substantial source of food for survival. But the hunting and trapping of animals for food and for other needs, such as clothing and tools, requires a great deal of prowess and patience. One must be trained to be a good hunter and trapper, and one must observe a certain code of conduct during that training. All life, from a tiny insect to a hot-tempered moose, has a sacred right to fulfill the measure of its creation, and in no way does this require that a beast become sport for man. Hunting for existence is a different proposition altogether and reflects a more serious and mature relationship with nature. Hunger is humbling, and killing creates a void on earth that is justified not by the desire for a shelf laden with trophies but rather by sincere need (Fig. 71).

Hunting an animal is a challenge, and if need is present, one can certainly enjoy that challenge. However, need implies putting the animal to good use; every part of it should be used for survival. To waste even a shred is inexcusable.

The methods used to obtain game in a primitive situation are varied, but many are cruel and should be avoided unless no other means presents itself.

Every resource for gathering in meat must be considered and used. If one puts all of his effort into hunting larger game, he usually ends up with only an empty stomach. Therefore, trapping small game and harvesting insects are a must in most areas. Hunting, then, should be second nature to the survivor, but it should not receive the main emphasis.

Insects

Some insects provide a lifesaving source of food in an emergency and can often be found in profusion after a hatch. If properly harvested, they can insure a food supply for several days. On the other hand, a survivor may have to be content with an occasional grub to add to his stew. When he forages, he should never disregard the lowly grasshopper because he thinks it is too insignificant to matter. The nutritional value of insects is high and adds substantially to a meager diet. However, *all insects must be cooked,* as they may harbor internal parasites that are very harmful to human beings. Further, one must be careful not to expend more energy harvesting food than the food can provide in return. Catching insects such as grasshoppers can be exasperating and tiring unless one learns a few tricks.

Listed here are some of the more common insects that provide good food. Also listed are appropriate methods of harvesting them and uses to which they can be put.

Grasshoppers, Locusts, Crickets, and Katydids; *Orthoptera*

Uses: If there are enough of these insects, they can be roasted and dried, ground into meal, and served in soups and stews. Smaller amounts can be boiled or roasted and served whole in soups and stews.

Harvesting Methods: At night grasshoppers climb tall plants and cling to the stalks near the top. They can be picked from the plants early in the morning while they are chilled and dormant. When grasshoppers are located in large numbers, several people can drive them with switches to one side of a meadow or clearing. The grasshoppers can then be swatted with willow switches. Grasshoppers and locusts in large numbers are available in some locales from late July until late August, usually in mountain meadows and plateau regions of the West.

Stone Flies and Other Nymphs; *Plecoptera*

Uses: Nymphs can be boiled in soups and stews with other food.

Harvesting Methods: Nymphs inhabit the undersides of stones in fast-moving streams, and they crawl on the water's edge in early spring. They are simply picked from stones and grass stems and stored in a wet container until they are needed for cooking.

Cicadas; *Homoptera*

Uses: The wings of the adult cicada are plucked, and then the insect is boiled in stew.

Harvesting Methods: Cicadas are found in juniper trees and brush in desert regions and can be harvested in the early morning in the same manner as grasshoppers. Cicadas can be located by the loud clicking noise they produce, somewhat similar to the sound of rattlesnakes.

Ants; *Hymenoptera*

Uses: Ants in quantity may be roasted, ground into powder, and added to soups and stews. When the ants are roasted, the abdomen usually separates from the rest of the body and can be winnowed as explained below to produce a sweet black sugar.

Harvesting Methods: Carpenter ants are found in dead trees and stumps and may be gathered by hand, as they are quite large. Small red and black ants build rather large mounds around areas of vegetation, constructing them from small sticks and other vegetable matter. One method of harvesting ants is to plant a deep container in the midst of a mound with the rim of the container level with the mound surface. When the den is stirred up, the ants fall into the container.

A more elaborate method, used by desert Indians, involves parching the ants. A whole den is first shoveled onto a winnowing tray made of willow shoots. Next, the whole tray is covered with a layer of hot coals. Then the tray is picked up and the entire mass is winnowed. The hot coals kill and roast the ants as they are gradually winnowed from the coals. During this process the mound dirt and chaff is also winnowed away.

Fig. 72. Skinning a rattlesnake.

Fig. 73. Bow and arrow used for frogs.

Fig. 74. Hunting with a frog bow.

Grubs and Caterpillars

Uses: There are many varieties of grubs and caterpillars that can be utilized in soups and stews, but those with hair or fuzz on them should be avoided as some are poisonous.

Harvesting Methods: Grubs are usually found in rotten logs and stumps, but seldom in large quantities. Caterpillars often infest a small area and can provide protein for several meals.

Reptiles and Amphibians

The best tool for snake hunting is a digging stick (Fig. 59). Making a special snake stick is a waste of time in a survival situation and just adds to the bulk of the gear. It is imperative that no one play with or tease a rattlesnake before killing it. After the snake is dead, its head should be cut off and buried. This is especially necessary if anyone in the group has bare feet.

All reptiles and amphibians should be skinned and eviscerated before they are cooked. Snakes and lizards are the most common reptiles, but at best they provide only meager sustenance for the amount of effort required to prepare them (Fig. 72). Frogs are a good source of nutrition, however, when they are found in quantity in marsh areas.

It is a simple matter to shoot frogs with three-pronged arrows and a crude bow. The arrows should be long—more like spears than arrows (Fig. 73). Reed grass and cattail spikes make the best shafts, but the foreshafts or prongs should be made from hardwood. For these, greasewood (*Sarcobatus*) is the finest. The bow does not need to be fancy, nor even very strong for this purpose. The distance for shooting frogs is rarely over three feet from the tip of the long arrow. The bow merely provides a speedier and more accurate propulsion than can be achieved by thrusting a spear with the arm. Even a green willow bow, cut and made on the spot, will do the job (Fig. 74).

Birds

Small birds should be considered as emergency food only, for efforts to obtain them are out of proportion to the amount of nourishment they provide.

Larger birds are worthy of one's closer attention, however, and in some areas they can provide substantial meat for the fire. Chucker partridge, quail, and sage hen are elusive targets even for a shotgun and are

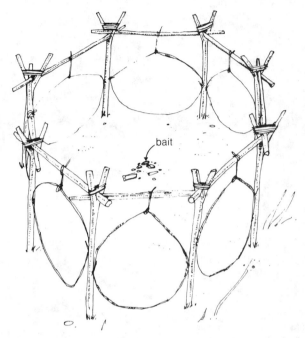

Fig. 75. Bird snares.

difficult to snare and trap. Yet, if the hunter is patient and prepared, he can capture these birds.

Sage hens can be hunted successfully with arrows or throwing sticks, and chuckers and quail can literally be herded along the ground in narrow canyons. These birds will not usually fly if they are not pressed too hard. Snares and nets can be set in the brush in areas that they frequent, and by making periodic drives, one can herd them into these traps (Fig. 75).

The Throwing Stick

More often called a rabbitstick, this device is not limited to rabbits. It is equally effective for all small game and birds. It is the universal hunting tool of most primitive tribes, ranging from a simple hardwood branch to a sophisticated boomerang. Generally, it is a flattened, curved stick shaped somewhat like a boomerang, but heavier and nonreturnable. A throwing stick glides and dips as it skims along the ground, taking up a swath as wide as the stick is long. It takes practice and a good arm to be effective (Figs. 76a–76c).

Fig. 76a. Throwing stick.

Fig. 76b. Preparing to throw the stick.

Fig. 76c. Correct release of throwing stick.

A throwing stick is my most trusted hunting tool. I have obtained more game with it than with any other primitive projectile weapon. Throwing sticks are simple in design and require minimal effort to make. Hardwood sticks can be cut while green with stone tools; split or scraped into shape with stone chips; hardened and cured in hot coals; and ready for use all in the same day. Fancier sticks require more curing time and extra polishing for better flying.

The final shape of a stick is governed by the shape of the branch you choose. The cross section is more important, however, and it is worthwhile to scrape carefully so that the stick turns out somewhat like an airplane wing—flat on the bottom and rounded on the top surface. The edges should be beveled to sharpness except at the handle end.

When throwing, it is best to hold the stick with the inside curve forward and step forward in a direct overhand throw. Just as you let go of the stick, give the wrist a little flick to the outside. This causes the stick to twist from flying end over end to flying in a wide-swathing spin parallel to the ground.

Deadfall Trapping

Deadfalls and snares are very effective for hunting animals, and trapping is one of the quickest and most humane ways to kill an animal if it is done responsibly. *However, the hunting of any game animal with traps and snares is forbidden except during an extreme emergency when one is lost in the wilderness.*

Responsible trapping implies competence, and every would-be trapper should be well acquainted with the best and most humane methods of trapping animals. Any trap that simply holds an animal is ranked lowest in effectiveness. Traps that kill quickly are ranked highest and should be considered first, if not exclusively, as the means of catching an animal.

Deadfalls are the most effective traps (Figs. 77-84). They kill instantly and usually without damage to the pelt. They are time-consuming to construct, but once in place they may be used indefinitely. With a quantity of lightweight triggers, a trapper may travel a great distance constructing the heavy parts of each trap from materials found in nature. Steel traps and snares are superior only if the area affords no natural materials for deadfalls. (For survival snares, see Figs. 85-89.)

Fig. 77. Paiute deadfall set.

Setting up and operating a deadfall trapline under survival conditions is quite different from operating a conventional trapline with steel traps. Many times students have reported to me that their traplines are too time-consuming to be effective because only six or seven good deadfalls can be set up in the late afternoon. Their problem is that they are not setting up deadfall lines according to a set-check pattern, which increases the number of sets each day until a good line of about one hundred traps are in operation. Set-check traplines work in the following way.

On the first day, construct as many triggers as you need for the entire line. This could range anywhere from fifty traps to two hundred, depending on your situation. Rarely can you catch enough to survive on with fewer than twenty traps. A hundred or more well-planned sets will provide plenty of meat and skins for survival. The size and strength of the triggers should be fairly standard, with a catch range geared to trip on a mouse as well as a fat rockchuck. Then, whether you make a set for a small or a medium-sized animal, your triggers will all be interchangeable. At least a few triggers should be larger and stronger and should be kept separate for the occasional opportunity to construct a set for larger animals like fox, coyote, or even bear. These animals are rare, however,

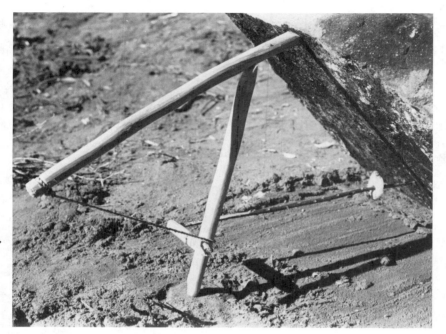

Fig. 78. Details of Paiute deadfall.

Fig. 79. Paiute deadfall trigger system.

and more meat can be obtained by trapping the more prolific and less cautious rodent populations.

When your triggers are all made, bundle them in groups of five and pack them for easy access on the trail.

Bait should be carefully planned and cared for. Many well-planned traplines have fallen short because of insufficient bait to finish out the line in an area where bait is scarce. For most rodents, anything salty or juicy will work as bait. A dough made from ground-up grass seeds or regular flour is best. Small chunks of hard fat, cooked meat, pine nuts, ripe cactus fruits, baked edible roots, and fresh dried bundles of hay made from clover, dandelion, or other succulent plants will also work.

The challenge in some cases is to keep from nibbling away at the bait yourself, before your traps are all out! When bait is unavailable, sets can be made to trip on contact using a bright object as a lure, or as a trail set through which an animal must pass to trip the set.

Placing one hundred deadfalls initially will take approximately three days of fairly constant effort. On day one, start the line up one side of a canyon or valley, concentrating on the most plentiful types of animals in the area, usually small rodents. Place your sets at frequent intervals and in places frequented by the animals. Check signs carefully to be sure they are not old and try to see a pattern of behavior in the animals' travels.

For instance, in the desert, large mice and rats are abundant. They establish runs along the bases of cliffs and rocky areas, but range out into the sandy areas for food gathering. It is obvious that the rocks afford the most protection, and if food were available there, the rodents would prefer to remain near that protection. Also, in the rocks they are less cautious and more liable to enter a deadfall set. Placing trap sets nearest their natural runways will therefore be more successful than open-ground sets near where they feed at night.

Try to construct each deadfall from stones found in the immediate area. This saves a lot of hard work and makes a less conspicuous set. Select the best possible site and make sure that the set is constructed in a permanent fashion. Any set that destroys itself upon its initial fall is not worth the effort. It must last through several successive settings. A firm base is essential and a permanent easy balance should be achieved. Rickety sets that need time-consuming balancing every time they are reset will be inefficient in the long run. When you take the time

trail

Fig. 80. Figure-4 trail deadfall. This is used on game trails where brush is thick and at entrances to burrows and dens. A V-shaped row of stakes fanning away from each approach causes game to go through rather than around the logs.

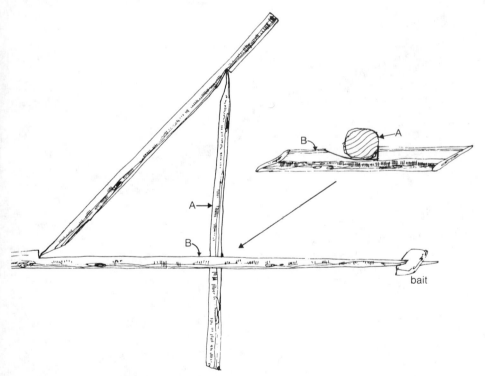

Fig. 81. Details of the figure-4 trap trigger.

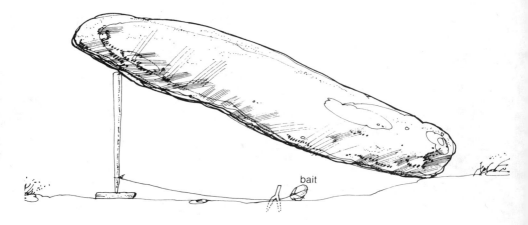

Fig. 82. Two-stick deadfall supporting a flat stone. This is simple to construct, but is not as effective as the figure-4 trap.

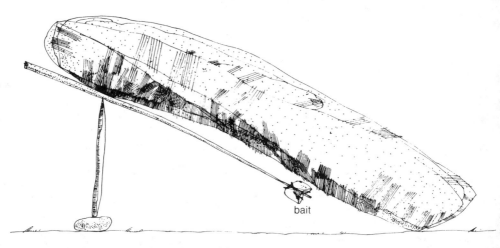

Fig. 83. Another type of two-stick deadfall.

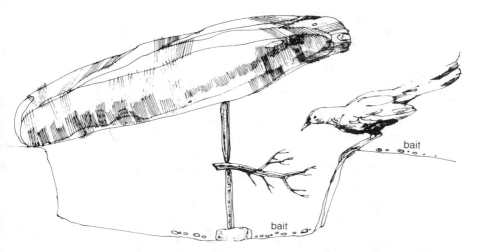

Fig. 84. Bird trap. The bird hops first onto the twig and causes the stone to fall. Rattlesnakes sometimes are caught with this; therefore, use caution when retrieving game.

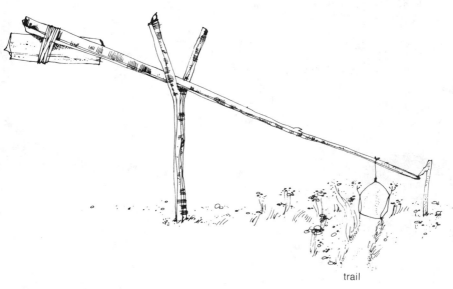

Fig. 85. Lift pole snare.

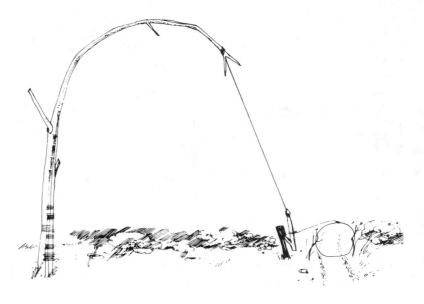

Fig. 86. Spring pole snare set on a trail.

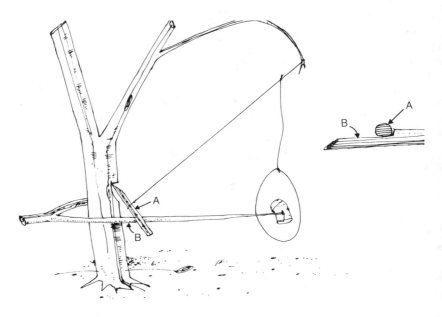

Fig. 87. Spring pole snare with baited trigger. The snare loop is placed where it will encircle the animal's neck as it reaches for the bait.

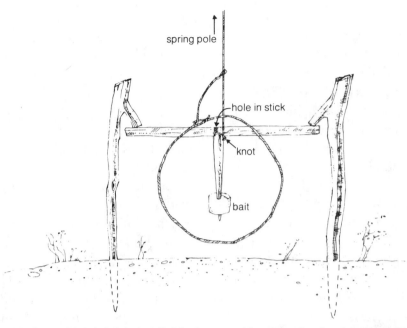

Fig. 88. Snare with bait. A hole is drilled in the cross stick and a string threaded through it with a knot in one end, and the bait stick is lightly forced into the hole so that the knot will not slip. A small fence is set up around one side so that the animal must reach through the snare loop to get the bait.

Fig. 89. Trail set snare placed in a feed run made by water animals. The animal drags the stone anchor into the water, sinks, and drowns. A float tied to the stone reveals the position of the snare after it sinks.

initially to shape the stone by knocking off an edge or building a firm base for it to rest on, you will save many hours later on. Fencing around deadfalls is essential and it should be well done. Natural materials from the immediate site are best.

Proceed in a definite pattern and direction in setting out the trapline. A careful accounting should be kept of where each set is located, and some signs should be left along the main trail, with small pebbles placed around it—one for each trap set in the immediate vicinity.

Approximately thirty traps can be set out in this fashion on the first day, in a line ranging from a mile to over five miles in length. It is best, however, to restrict the range to less than three miles, or about ten traps per mile. In areas where small animals are abundant, as many as thirty traps may be effective over and over again in a short one-mile stretch. This reduces the time needed to check them and saves energy as well.

On the morning of the second day, quickly check your first thirty traps. Reset the tripped sets, improve those needing improvement, and return to camp with your catch. Process the catch, eat, and then travel up the opposite side of the canyon or valley, setting out another thirty or forty deadfalls.

Early on the third morning, check all the traps, process the catch, eat, and repeat the pattern of the second day. This time, though, set the rest of your traps near areas where good catches were made during the previous two days. This insures a greater yield in the days to come without extending the area of the trapline. From that point on, the line is maintained by checking it each morning, resetting the traps that are sprung, and processing the catch. This can all be done in about three hours if the trapline is not over three miles long. Time should be taken to pull traps that do not produce and construct sets in a new location if necessary. A few extra replacement triggers should always be carried, along with new bait. Some sets will fall on their triggers and break them.

Trapping is the surest way to get meat in a survival situation. The trapline will bring you ample food for your effort in the long run, since it is working for you while you are sleeping. That kind of economy can't be beat. The major daytime tasks of gathering plant foods, hunting, drying meat, and doing other chores are not seriously disrupted by a trapline that is checked early in the morning.

Hunting and Stalking

Using primitive weapons to capture game is extremely different from shooting with a rifle at a deer as it runs across the canyon. In a survival situation a person must exercise all of his ability in order to get close enough to his prey for his arrows or spear to be effective (Fig. 90). But stalking deer and other large game is not difficult if the following techniques are mastered:

- The hunter must spot the deer before it sees him.
- He must keep downwind from the deer.
- He must watch the deer's feeding habits until a pattern is observed. Most deer feed for about twenty seconds and then raise their heads for a look around. When their heads are down, they see nothing but the brush they are eating.

Fig. 90. Hunting with a primitive bow and arrow.

- The hunter must slowly walk toward the animal when its head is down. As he walks he counts to ten and then stops. He must never press his luck by trying to gain a few more steps before the deer looks up, for it might catch him in the middle of a step. The hunter should make no attempt to hide; instead, he should relax in place, because the wait might be a long one. In a few seconds the deer will raise its head and survey the country but will see only movement. When it looks in the direction of the hunter it might gaze at him for some time, but if the hunter does not even so much as bat an eyelash, the deer will soon ignore him and continue feeding.

- The hunter should walk forward again for another count of ten as soon as the deer drops its head, and then freeze, continuing this procedure until the range is right for a good shot. Somehow a deer fails to comprehend that what appears to be an old stump is closer every time the deer looks up.

Deer can also be ambushed at water holes during early dawn hours or in the late evening. The secret here is for the hunter to conceal himself in a spot that does not allow the deer to sense his presence and yet does allow a clear shot. Two or more people can drive deer past hunters concealed along well-used deer trails.

Another technique consists of the hunter calling the animal to him. If he, for instance, learns to mimic the cry of a mouse or rabbit in pain, the hunter will be able to attract any carnivore as well as the animal he imitates. There are a number of ways to make good animal calls, but the simplest and perhaps the finest involves only the lips and the back of the hand. A long, drawn-out kiss on the back of a wet hand sounds (with practice) like a squalling rabbit or mouse. Short smacks sound like the call of a chipmunk or rockchuck. With a little practice a hunter can develop a number of calls using only the lips and hands (Fig. 91).

Rockchucks and ground squirrels may easily be fooled by two hunters who make an open approach to the animal's den as one of them whistles a lively tune. When the animal dives for his hole, the hunters continue walking, and the whistler, still whistling, walks on by and off into the distance. The other hunter quickly conceals himself in a position for a good shot and then waits. The rockchuck, hearing the whistling fading in the distance, comes out for a look around; if the concealed hunter is a good shot, he has himself a meal (Fig. 92).

Fig. 91. Calling Game.

Fig. 92. Using the primitive Indian technique.

Fig. 93. Using a rodent skewer.

Sometimes a rodent can be dragged from its den with a rodent skewer, a simple device made from a long supple willow with a small fork in one end (Fig. 93). The hunter thrusts it into the hole until he feels the animal. Then, by gently twisting the stick, he catches the forked end in the animal's fur and winds it tightly. As he gently pulls and coaxes, he brings the rodent to the surface.

Ground squirrels and mice can be caught by flooding them from their holes with a diverted stream or with buckets of water. They can be killed with sticks as they emerge.

Fish

Catching fish can be difficult in outdoor survival, but a few techniques can provide enough for a tasty meal.

Tackle

Making fishing tackle requires some special skills in working bone and in twisting fibers for line. The fibers best suited for this are stinging nettle (*Urtica*), milkweed (*Asclepias*), dogbane (*Apocynum cannabinum*), and the bark of the haw tree (*Crataegus*). They must be selected carefully and twisted tightly (see Cordage in Chapter 7). Ten feet of line on a long willow pole will serve well in most rivers and streams.

Hooks are best made of bone. The simplest is the skewer hook, which is a sliver of bone that is tied at the middle, turned parallel to the line, and inserted into the bait (Fig. 94). When the fish swallows the bait, the bone turns sideways and holds. Another simple device is the cross hook, where the crosspiece is turned parallel to the main shank when the bait is applied. When the fish swallows this, the crosspiece is pulled sideways, the hook is set, and the fish is caught (Fig. 95).

Conventional hooks can be made of bone in the following manner:

- A small thin-walled bone (only bird and rodent bones will do) is selected and cut into a rectangle.

- The piece of bone is then drilled several times so that the center portion can be removed.

- The partitions between the drill holes are removed with a stone or bone punch and the walls are smoothed with a small piece of sanding stone. The result is a rectangular ring of bone.

Fig. 94. Skewer hook made from bone.

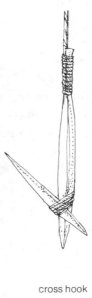 

cross hook   baited

Fig. 95. Cross hook made from bone.

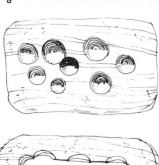

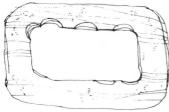

Fig. 96. Making hooks from bird bone.

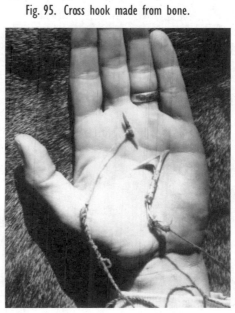

Fig. 97. Attaching hooks to line.

■ The ring is then cut in two places, and the result is two hooks, which must be sharpened and then attached to a lead line (Fig. 96).

Hooks are attached to the line by a tight wrapping of fine string or fiber. The hook shank is first notched and then smeared with pitch or some other sticky substance. After the wrapping is attached, it is sealed to the hook with pitch. Hooks can be successfully tied onto the line without pitch, however, if the wrapping is made tight in the notches (Fig. 97).

Wishbones of small birds may also be used for hooks (Fig. 98).

It is extremely difficult to catch trout and other game fish in small streams with this crude equipment, but river fish such as carp, suckers, catfish, chubs, redhorse, squawfish, and whitefish are easily caught and prove to be very tasty when fried or baked.

Traps

A good fish trap will catch many more fish than a hook and line. There are several different types, all of which are good. Traps are best built and placed according to the nature of the stream or river—ingenuity in using natural features to aid in making and setting the traps will largely determine their success (Figs. 99–101).

Spears

Many fish feed in shallow water and are easily caught with a simple spear made from a willow rod about fourteen feet long to which is bound a set of hardwood prongs. The prongs should be bound with most of their length attached to the shaft, as this will insure the sturdiness of the device when it is used roughly. Few fish are lost if they are speared through the side and then pinned to the bottom by quickly pushing the spear into an upright position and forcing it into the mud (Figs. 102, 103).

There are several other types of spears that can be used. However, none of them will serve any better than the simple one mentioned above. It might prove interesting to try them when time warrants the effort to manufacture them (Fig. 104).

Fig. 98. Hook made from wishbone of a small bird.

Fig. 99. Willow fish trap placed in stream riffles between pools.

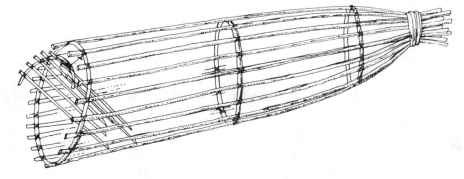

Fig. 100. Willow fish trap. A V-shaped barrier fence made of willows stuck in mud leading to the opening will direct migrating fish into the trap.

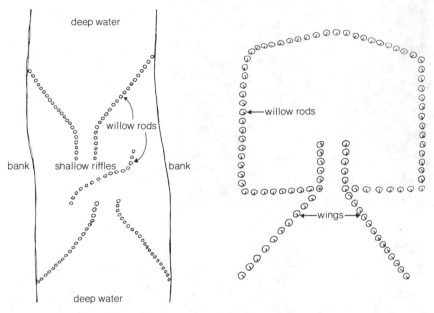

Fig. 101. Winged fish traps. These are made from willow rods driven into a stream bottom. Numerous variations of this trap are possible in most shallow streams and rivers.

Other Water Life

A good part of wild animal food sources lives in or near the water, and much of it is so easily caught that a person could live indefinitely from one small stream. Crayfish, mussels, helgramites, stone flies, snails, minnows, and polliwogs are the most common and are found under rocks and moss or mud along the shore. Crayfish and mussels are the most desirable and can be gathered in fairly large quantities. Mussels are sometimes found buried in the mud—a shallow trail terminating in a slight hump in the mud will betray their presence. In shallow, gravel-covered stream bottoms, they are found sticking up among the rocks. Just feel for them. Crayfish appear in the evening and can be caught by hand or with a hook and line. They can be scared out by moving the rocks that cover them, but they must be grabbed quickly and carefully.

A willow basket trap placed in a swift-flowing stream will net crayfish, small fish, and a multitude of other water life if a proper drive is made. The survivor can do this by situating the trap so that it faces upstream and then staking it to the bottom or having another person hold it

Fig. 102. Making a fish spear from a willow.

Fig. 103. Preparing to spear a fish.

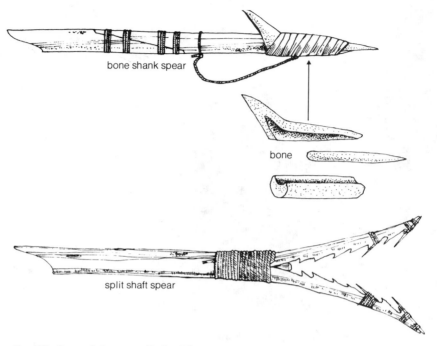

bone shank spear

bone

split shaft spear

Fig. 104. Some of the most effective fish spears.

securely. Then, entering the water twenty or thirty feet upstream, he begins kicking and scuffing rocks and gravel and slowly works his way downstream toward the trap. He moves every stone and stirs the bottom vigorously, then raises the trap, removes the catch, and places the trap in a new location. This technique often produces buckets of incredible edibles.

Jerky

Meat will not keep very long in warm weather; therefore, it is necessary to dry any surplus for future use. The standard modern methods of making jerky involve brines and spices that give the meat a rich flavor. However, these processes decrease food value and render the meat so salty that a substantial meal of nothing but jerky would make a person sick.

Meat jerked for use as a food rather than as a snack or delicacy must be prepared without brines and spices. It is merely cut into thin strips about one-fourth inch thick and dried in the sun for a couple of days.

When it becomes hard and brittle, it is taken down and stored in a pit or in bags. It is then used in stews and soups or roasted lightly on the coals and eaten (Fig. 105).

Cutting meat into strips may be difficult when small chunks are involved; it is easiest to take a chunk and cut through it to within one-quarter inch of the other side. Then, by turning the knife sideways, the chunk can be cut or unrolled into a long strip for drying (Fig. 106).

Small animals and birds can be dried whole. After they are skinned and eviscerated and after the back is cracked between the legs, a stick is inserted to hold the body cavity open. The animals are then laid on rocks in the sun to dry. When thoroughly dried, they are pounded until

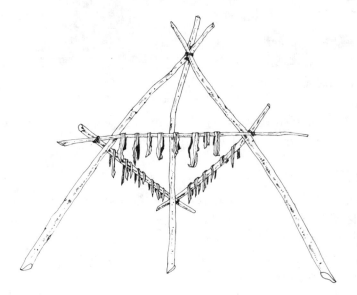

Fig. 105. Jerky hung out to dry.

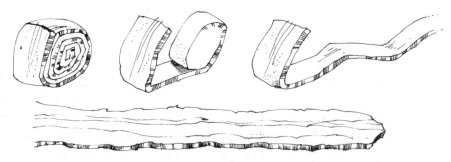

Fig. 106. Cutting or unrolling jerky.

Fig. 107. Ground squirrel spread out to dry in the sun.

the bones are crushed. Another day in the sun will dry the marrow and insure preservation (Figs. 107, 108).

Pemmican

Pemmican, a mixture that surpasses the taste and nutrition of K rations, is made with berries that have been dried to remove the excess moisture and then pounded into a paste. Dried pounded jerky is added to this paste, and then melted suet is mixed with the berries and meat. The mixture is next rolled into small balls and stored in the cleaned intestines of a large animal. The intestine sack is tied shut, sealed with suet, and stored in a cool, dry place. Pemmican prepared in this way will keep for several months (Fig. 109). Balls of pemmican are also safely stored in plastic bags or leather bags that are richly soaked in melted suet.

Dried Fish

Small minnows are easily dried when spread out in the sun, and it is not necessary to clean them. But larger minnows over two and one-half inches long should be eviscerated and split for drying. The sun will dry

Fig. 108. Pounding jerky.

Fig. 109. Pemmican ready for eating.

small fish in one to two days, after which they can be put into bags for safekeeping or placed in a storage pit for preservation.

Drying larger fish is accomplished in one of two ways. The simplest is to split the fish down the back and hang it on a rack. This way the bones are still intact and make eating difficult, but one can get around this by pounding the dried fish into a fine meal to be used in stews. This crushes the larger bones, and the finer ones are softened by cooking.

A second method is to fillet the fish and dry the strips by hanging them on a rack in the sun. One cuts the meat from the bones after splitting the fish down the back and removing the side strips by slicing along the ribs. There is some waste if the bones are not saved, however. In a survival situation waste is not tolerable. The remaining bones can be used well if they are dried slightly and then ground into a meal to be added to stews.

All dried fish will keep a year or more if it is stored in a dry place. Eating dried fish is not always a pleasant experience at first, and the possibility of parasites always exists. For these reasons it is best to cook the fish before eating it.

The advantage of pounding or grinding fish is that this allows the fish to dry more thoroughly, minimizing the risk of spoilage and reducing the space taken up by bulky chunks. The fish meal has many more uses than whole strips—it can be used in breads, soups, stews, and stuffings; mixed with cooked seed grains for a wholesome cereal; and moistened, made into patties, and fried.

Fig. 110. Hafted stone knives.

Special Skills

In an outdoor survival situation, people can use only the natural materials around them for constructing tools; therefore, they must know how to use nature's materials effectively (Fig. 110). The following explanations of a few of the more important methods of making and using primitive tools will be helpful, but common sense and the realization that many other methods will also work is the key.

The skills discussed here are presented exactly as I have used them while living off the land. They appear in this order: working stone, working bone, constructing bows and arrows, constructing atlatls and spears, making cordage, preparing sinew, weaving sandals and baskets, making rawhide, and tanning skins.

Working Stone

To accomplish the tasks of cutting, digging, scraping, chopping, and building, ancient peoples developed a remarkable array of tools made from stone. The skills required to produce such workable tools are more complex than one might imagine and show evidence of a high degree of inventiveness and manual dexterity. The amount of work that can be done with these tools is remarkable.

A person thrown into a primitive survival situation would quickly find his existence greatly impaired without the aid of so simple a tool as a pocketknife. It would seem that one could never survive without a knife to cut poles for building shelters, to cut shafts for a spear or bow, or to fashion the myriad items essential for survival. The construction of almost everything requires the direct or indirect use of a cutting or chopping edge, which is itself fashioned with implements made with cutting and chopping tools (Figs. 111, 112).

The more common methods of working stone that are discussed here I carefully researched and repeatedly tested until I achieved mastery of them.

The process of shaping stone can be divided into four major methods: (1) percussion flaking, (2) pressure flaking, (3) pecking or crumbling, (4) abrading. Other recognized methods such as incising and piercing are minor and can be considered as variations of the abrading process under special conditions. They are used exclusively to shape very soft rocks such as soapstone.

Percussion Flaking

Percussion flaking, a highly technical art demanding precise skill and forethought, consists of three techniques: (1) direct percussion with a hammerstone, (2) indirect percussion with a hammerstone and a punch, and (3) direct or indirect percussion with the stone resting on another larger stone (anvil). All three techniques can be used in producing a single tool.

Direct percussion, also called direct freehand percussion, can be used for shaping large pieces of rock into blanks from which specialized tools can be fashioned. In practice, the stone to be shaped is held in the left hand and fractured with blows from a hammerstone or horn baton held in the right hand. Simple axes and choppers can be made in this manner from common rhyolite or quartzite cobbles. The blows of the hammerstone should fall directly onto the edge of the core, especially if it is a rather thin one. This is necessary for working chert, coarse agate, dull jasper, or any other nonglassy stone. Holding the blank at an angle while striking off chips is often necessary for removing rough spots and trimming edges. For instance, obsidian and other similar glassy rock cannot be chipped successfully if it is struck directly on the edge of the core. The core must be struck at an angle if crumbling edges and unwanted hinge fractures are to be avoided (Fig. 113).

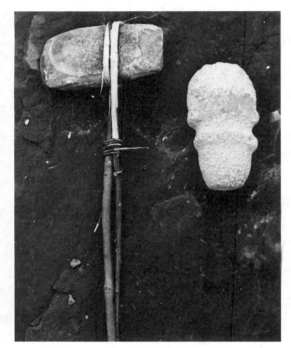

Fig. 111. Chopping tools.

Fig. 112. Cutting tools.

Fig. 113. Striking flakes. (a) Striking directly into hard shale or cobblestone; (b) Striking glassy rock (obsidian or jasper) at an angle with the hammerstone; (c) Striking flakes from glassy stones incorrectly; (d) Striking flakes by indirect percussion.

Fig. 114. Striking the core with an antler baton.

Fig. 115. A blade struck from the core.

When cutting blades or other specialized tools are needed, a striking platform must be constructed on the core. This is done by merely breaking a rock in half, leaving two cores, each with one flat surface. Striking blades from the core is then relatively easy. If the stroke carries all the way through the core, good blades will be produced consistently. If the core is worked around with even strokes, a number of razor-sharp blades can be made before the core is exhausted (Figs. 114, 115).

If a blank has a difficult knob or thick edge in such a place as to make direct percussion impractical, it can be worked down individually with the aid of a punch made from deer antler or other antler of similar density. This process requires the assistance of a second person. The blank is held in the left hand, which is protected with a leather pad, and the punch is placed against the edge of the blank and steadied with the other hand. The assistant then strikes the punch sharply with a hammerstone. In this way the force is applied to the exact spot intended.

Percussion flaking with the blank resting on another stone (anvil) works but is rarely necessary except for removing troublesome knobs and for striking off larger flakes to thin down a thick blank. For this it is best to use the indirect percussion method with the blank resting on a padded anvil.

A variation of the indirect percussion method calls for the blank to be placed between the knees with the edge to be flaked facing up. One person can then use the punch and hammerstone without an assistant. There is no danger that the chips will cut the knees if the blank is placed in the fold of a thick piece of leather. Variations of this sort are numerous among modern flint workers and were probably just as numerous in aboriginal times. Using one method instead of another is purely a matter of preference. Basically, using the hammerstone or antler baton to shape tools is the most practical form of percussion flaking.

Pressure Flaking

The more delicate job of finishing a blank into a specialized implement requires the simplest of tools but a complex nervous system. A nervous Indian probably spent more time bandaging his cuts than making arrowheads. A piece of antler and a leather pad are all that is needed for producing the finest knives and arrowpoints (Fig. 116). A blank or blade produced by percussion flaking or a simple chip of flint or obsidian is held in the palm of the left hand with the fingers gripping it firmly. A leather pad protects the hand from being cut. The hand is braced against the left knee, and small chips are pressed off the blank with the antler flaker. The tip of the antler is placed on the edge of the flint and pressure is applied inward and downward against it. At the same time, a slight twist is applied to the antler, causing the chip to come off the underside of the blank. Considerable skill is required for superior results, but one can turn out serviceable tools in a short time with only a little practice (Fig. 117).

The following tips will be helpful for the beginner:

- When the stone is gripped in one hand, it must be held slightly forward on the heel of the hand and braced against the knee, so that pressure from the fingers will tip the edge up. This allows the flaker tip to force the chip off the bottom side of the blank. Failure to hold the stone properly can result in the quick reduction of the number of fingers on the hand of even the most skilled Stone Age artisan.

- The power of the wrist is not sufficient for flaking larger pieces of stone, so that the force applied with the tip of the flaker must come from the weight of the body. The push should be fairly hard but not sudden. The best results are achieved by just leaning the body into the tip of the flaker with a steady, even pressure. Sudden hard lunges can cause loss of control and often result in bad cuts.

- The tip of the flaker should not be sharpened to a fine point but given a blunt chisel shape. This allows it to grip the blank firmly.

Fig. 116. Pressure flaking with an antler and a pad.

- The force is applied in the direction in which the flake should run. The objective is to make the flake run across the bottom face of the blank. If the tool is pushed downward at a ninety-degree angle, the flake will be short and stubby.

- The flake comes off more readily if the force of the flaker, as it is applied against the edge of the blank, is accompanied by a slight twist.

The method of pressure flaking described above is the most widely used. One variation uses a stone anvil as a rest and is similar to indirect rest percussion. The difference is that instead of the flakes being struck off, they are pressed off with the punch. Here again, individual preference is the rule. All of the possible methods and techniques for percussion and pressure flaking can be combined and modified to accomplish the task of flaking stone into useful tools.

Antler and leather are the usual tools for pressure flaking, but only the student trained with civilized exactness would fail to improvise suitable substitutes. The archaic craftsman caught without his chipping kit would replace the leather with a pad of sagebrush bark, a flat piece of tree bark, or some green moss. In place of the antler he might use a bone or tooth fragment set in a wooden handle. He might even use a hardwood stick or a sliver of rock, though these do not work as well. The importance of being able to improvise with materials and techniques cannot be overestimated.

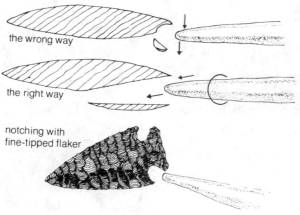

the wrong way

the right way

notching with
fine-tipped flaker

Fig. 117. Details of pressure flaking.

Pecking or Crumbling

Shaping stones by crumbling them requires relatively little brain power but a lot of perseverance and resignation to monotony. A caveman working stone probably often reached the nervous-breakdown point when he shattered his newly finished axehead with that final perfectionist's tap. I can almost hear the canyons ringing with whatever verbal abuses left his lips.

The king of stoneworking implements, the hammerstone, is all that is needed for pecking or crumbling. With it and infinite patience, colossal stelae and monumental blocks of solid stone have been shaped for temples and other buildings. However, primitive man for the most part was content to use the hammerstone to make axes, clubheads, mortars and pestles, metates and manos, and various other necessary items (Fig. 118).

Hammerstones are best made from quartzite cobbles and can have a number of different shapes and sizes. To use them, one has only to start pecking away at another rock, preferably one that is slightly softer than the hammerstone. The strokes should be even and rapid and not too hard, and they should be kept up until the surface of the stone being

Fig. 118. Using the hammerstone.

Fig. 119. Sharpening an axehead.

shaped starts to crumble away into a fine dust. The rock being shaped should never rest on a solid surface as it will crack under the blows of the hammerstone. It should be held loosely in the hand. In this way the tool slowly takes shape. The crumbling process can be speeded up by applying water to the crumbling surface. Axes are generally roughly shaped by percussion flaking with the hammerstone before they are subjected to the crumbling process. A good axehead can be turned out in about an hour, and another hour of grinding and polishing will give it the touch of beauty found in the finest southwestern stonework (Fig. 119).

One can easily haft an axe by heating a slender willow, wrapping it twice around the axehead, and securing it in place by wrapping it with willow shoots or cord. This type of axe handle will hold tightly and withstand a good deal of abuse (Figs. 120, 121). This method of hafting axes is unequaled for efficiency and ease of handling.

Abrading

Grinding, cutting, sawing, drilling, scraping, whetting, rasping, and polishing are all part of the abrading process. Abrasion is especially important

Fig. 120. Wrapping the handle on.

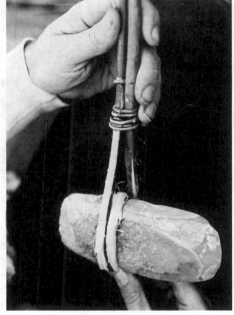

Fig. 121. Completing hafting of the axehead.

in shaping and finishing stones to be used in food preparation, because the smoothing of these implements reduces the amount of grit that is shed into foodstuffs. The cutting edges of implements made of granular stones such as basalt and slate can be honed to perfection by abrasion.

Grinding and whetting stone simply requires another stone upon which the implement is rubbed. The best abrading stones are sandstone and other granular rocks that contain hard pieces of silica. Sand poured on the surface of the abrading stone is an effective abrasive, and pouring or dribbling water over the surface speeds up the process. Even the hardest agates can be ground and polished if they are rubbed against a simple abrasive. Like the crumbling process, successful abrasion takes mostly time and patience. Except for honing cutting edges and smoothing food-grinding implements, grinding and polishing stone are largely used to give a finished look to tools that are already serviceable.

Fig. 123. Using the pump drill.

Fig. 122. Chopping a willow sapling with the axe.

Cutting or sawing stone is accomplished not with a toothed stone saw but by abrasion with thin slabs of an abrasive stone. Jade and other tough materials can be beautifully carved and grooved with simple slab saws and the use of sand and water as abrasive agents.

Drilling stone is accomplished in a number of ways, but the most common consists of a pump drill with a stone bit. The bit must be made of very hard material, jasper and agate being the finest. With a good pump drill it is a simple matter to drill slate, chert, basalt, rhyolite, or any other soft stone. Even hard stone can in time be penetrated if fine quartz sand is used as the abrasive. Water speeds up the drilling process, but it must be replenished repeatedly, and the hole must be kept clean and rinsed out or grit will form a thick paste in it and choke up the drill (Fig. 123).

A simpler drill consists of a simple stick with a stone bit. This device is twirled between the hands. The simplest drill is merely a bit grasped in the fingers and twisted back and forth into the material being drilled.

Stone bits are usually necessary for getting the hole started. But after a shallow hole is formed in the stone, a bone or hardwood bit can be substituted, with sand serving as an abrasive. Bone and wood bits grip the grains of sand, causing them to cut rapidly into the stone. Water cannot be used with a wooden drill bit as it causes the wood to swell and bind.

Stone Versus Steel

Comparing primitive stone tools to modern tools of steel leaves little doubt as to which is superior. At the same time, stone tools cannot be dismissed as worthless or ineffective. Flint arrowheads are entirely equal to steel heads in their penetrating power; stone axeheads, though somewhat slower, will cut down a tree with as much sureness as the finest steel axe; a stone drill bit will make as neat a hole as a high-carbon steel bit; and a flint knife will skin a deer and cut it up as well as a modern butcher knife.

Thus, it seems reasonable to some artisans dedicated to primitive skills that mastery of the techniques of the Stone Age is imperative to true outdoor survival. The survivor can be master of any situation and need not fear the loss of any implement if he can successfully apply the stoneworking techniques described in this chapter.

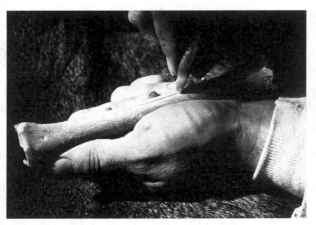

Fig. 124. Scratching a groove with the graver.

Working Bone

Cutting and carving bone into useful implements presents some special problems when one is working with stone tools only. But the following tips on handling bone-working implements will greatly reduce the time and sweat required to make a simple bone tool:

- For splitting bone, the tool of value is a graver, which one can make easily by flaking a small sharp nipple on the edge of a piece of hard stone, preferably agate or jasper. It is used to scratch a light groove down the length of a bone. The cut is then deepened with the application of rapid strokes made with the graver tip, the groove serving as a guide channel. This process is repeated on the opposite side of the bone. Next the bone is placed on a stone and tapped with a small rock. The tapping is repeated all along the edges of the grooves until the bone splits (Figs. 124–126).

- For notching bone, a stoneflake is needed. Notches in a bone tool permit one to tie on strings or carve out jagged edges, and these are easily created with a stoneflake.

- For sharpening and honing bone, a sanding stone is required (Fig. 127). The bone is rubbed back and forth on a rough stone surface and finished on a finer sanding stone. Small pieces of bone can be ground between two sanding surfaces. As the two stones are rubbed back and forth, the bone between them is ground rapidly.

- For drilling bone, the process is exactly as for drilling stone (see above).

Fig. 125. Tapping a grooved bone with a small rock.

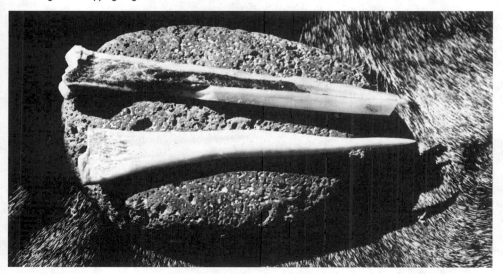

Fig. 126. Split bone and finished awl made from a split bone.

Fig. 127. Sharpening a bone awl with a sanding stone.

Constructing Bows and Arrows

An archer under primitive conditions is somewhat different from the modern bowman with his laminated finery. Even at best, his equipment is vastly inferior, so that his success in hunting depends more on patience, practice, good luck, and a keen stalking ability that allows him close shots. But the value of the primitive bow and arrow must never be underestimated, as they are an important aid in filling the stewpot. The perfect shot quite often presents itself in the wilderness, and the wise hunter has something to take it with (Figs. 128, 129).

Bows

The finest woods for making bows include mountain mahogany (*Cercocarpus*), ash (*Fraxinus*), serviceberry (*Amelanchier*), and chokecherry (*Prunus*). A sapling burned by a brushfire is excellent bow wood. Many trees uprooted by wind also have well-seasoned branches. But a dead tree with its roots still in the ground may be too brittle or too weathersplit for use, unless it has been killed by fire.

Since preseasoned wood is rare in the wilderness, green wood usually has to fill the need, and if carefully cured it is superior to other woods. A straight stave that is free from knots and small branches should be selected, and the stave should be carefully cut clear through, not broken off. It is the wise survivor who selects two or three staves to work with—an extra bow stuck in the belt is good insurance. The bow described here is a "quickie bow" made in the style of the African Bushmen. Flat Native American bows are better, but take more time in a survival situation.

The measurements of a bow will vary with the available wood supply, but too often staves are selected that are too large in diameter. The best diameter is from one to two inches at the handgrip. This must be determined *before* the bark is removed.

The bow length should be approximately forty-four inches, but this will vary with each person. A good method of determining bow length is to hold the stave on a horizontal plane extending from the left shoulder to the fingertips of the extended right arm.

Once the staves are selected and measured, the bark should be scraped off and the staves left overnight in a cool, dry place. The staves must not be exposed to sunlight for the first six hours after the bark is removed.

Fig. 128. Taking a shot.

Fig. 129. Finished bow and arrows.

The process of shaping a bow requires more than skill; it demands sensitivity and patience as well. Every stave, no matter how straight, has a natural bend to it that can be determined by placing the butt end on the ground and holding the stave vertical with the left hand in the middle, where the handgrip will be. The bowmaker grasps the tip of the stave with the right hand and pulls it toward him lightly. The stave will turn in his left hand and settle into its natural bend. The side of the stave facing away from him then becomes the back of the bow (Fig. 130).

Only after the bend is determined should the actual shaping of the bow commence. Holding the stave with the butt, or larger, end down, one can determine the exact position for the center of the handgrip and mark it with a scratch. Next trim the upper half of the bow to the exact dimensions desired, completing the top before starting on the lower half. The danger in completing the lower half first is that one will scrape away too much wood, causing the top half of the bow to be too narrow and fragile and perhaps making the diameter at the handgrip too narrow. If the top half of the bow is finished to the exact dimensions desired, the bottom half will be relatively easy to shape, with plenty of wood to work with and little danger of trimming away too much.

Trimming the bow stave to its final dimensions should be done by sight alone. Each half is gracefully tapered from the center to the end in an even plane that results in a pointed tip. The circumference should be kept round from the handgrip to both tips of the bow. If the diameter turns out somewhat larger than expected, the belly of the bow can be flattened, but only to the degree that the bow becomes more flexible along its entire length.

The bow should never be drawn to test it during its construction. Testing can be done by bending the bow *slightly* at intervals and judging its strength or stiffness by sight and weight. A good bow will look good and will be graceful and light.

The actual trimming and shaping should not be done by whittling. Rather, the excess wood should be scraped off in long even strokes from the handgrip to the tips (Fig. 131). A piece of flint, agate, jasper, or obsidian does the best job, but broken glass and steel knife blades are also effective. However, the bowmaker using a steel knife blade is often strongly tempted to speed up the process by whittling with it, and this ruins a bow stave. Most staves cut in the wilderness catch the blade and

Fig. 130. Determining the natural bend of the bow.

Fig. 131. Scraping the bow stave.

Fig. 132. Planing the bow with a flint chip.

guide the cut in a spiral, causing the carver to remove too much wood in a small area and to make an uneven taper.

Holding a stone blade with sharp edges at a right angle to the stave, one can shave off thin strips of wood much as one would when using a plane (Fig. 132). This tool is sometimes called a planar scraper or a flake blade (Fig. 133).

When the bow is finished it should be stored away for a day or two to cure. The curing process can be speeded up by holding the bow over hot coals or standing it by the fire.

When the bow is dry it should be greased with all the animal fat it can absorb. The survivor should then heat the bow and rub it until his arm aches. Fat can be obtained from any animal, even a mouse, or fish oil can be obtained from several chopped and boiled fish. The oil is skimmed off the water surface and rubbed on the bow. If no oil is available, the bow can be used as it is.

Once during a survival expedition I was severely criticized by my companions and made to walk downwind from them for braving the stench of an old deer carcass to obtain some sinew and a chunk of rancid fat. However, they envied my efforts several days later when I completed a fine bow of serviceberry wood and used the fat and sinew to finish it off. We were miles away from the deer carcass by then and they gratefully shared my treasure for their own bows. After that we all smelled the same.

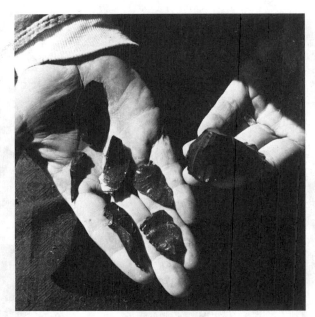

Fig. 133. Planar scrapers and flake blades.

Fig. 134. Recurving the bow tips.

Fig. 135. Roughening the bow tips.

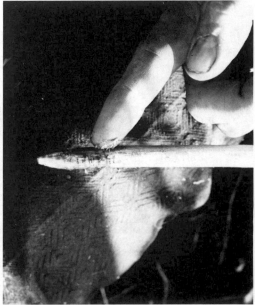

Fig. 136. Smearing pitch on the bow tips.

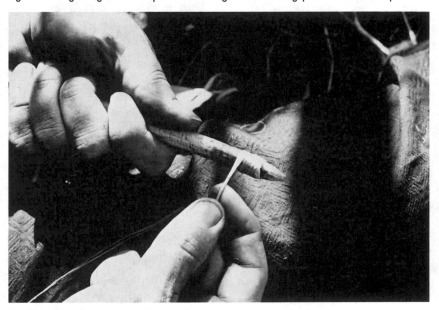

Fig. 137. Wrapping sinew on the bow tips.

After the bow is cured and greased, the survivor can give it a final shaping by recurving the tips. This involves heating each tip over hot coals and then bending it over a smooth, round stone, holding it in position until it cools (Fig. 134).

The tips can be notched to receive the bowstring or left smooth. Smooth tips help prevent splitting, but to be sure they hold the bowstring securely, they should be scratched with a flint chip to roughen the surface. Then the tips are smeared with hot, boiled pine pitch and wrapped with sinew from the tip down about three inches (Figs. 135–137). This provides a no-slip surface to tie the bowstring to and further helps to prevent the tips of the bow from splitting.

To string the bow, tie the bowstring permanently to the sinew at one end and wrap it around the other end two or three times, securing it with two half hitches (Fig. 138).

The bow is now complete. It should be shot with the stave held on the same plane in which it originally grew—the butt end pointing down and the narrower tip up. It should be kept unstrung when not in use and greased regularly (Fig. 139).

In a survival situation, a quickie bow like this will do the job admirably for a skilled and patient hunter. If all the materials are available, it

Fig. 138. Stringing the bow.

Fig. 139. Finished bow.

can be made in no more than two days. Primitive artisans usually spent a great deal more time than this and consequently produced longer-lasting but not necessarily more effective equipment. This bow is capable of killing large game as well as rabbits, squirrels, and birds. But it is only as effective as its maker and user.

Bowstrings

The strongest bowstrings are made from sinew (see Preparing Sinew later in this chapter), but nettle, milkweed, and some barks are usable though inferior substitutes. The string should be at least twelve inches longer than the bow.

Sinew strands are twisted together for the bowstring as follows. Hold two strands of sinew in the left hand, pinching them together between the thumb and second joint of the forefinger. The strand that is farthest from the body is then tightly twisted a few turns clockwise with the right hand. Fold the twisted strand counterclockwise over the other strand. Now the twisted strand is the one closest to the body. Take the untwisted strand and twist it tightly a few turns clockwise, then folding it back over the first strand as before. The tighter the sinew is twisted, the finer and thinner the cord will be.

Fig. 140. Proper position for holding sinew.   Fig. 141. Twisting counterclockwise.

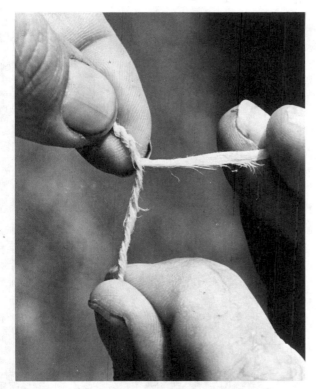

Fig. 142. Folding the twisted strand over the other strand.

Fig. 143. Adding new strands to the cord.

Fig. 144. Twisting in the new strands.

Fig. 145. Preparing reeds for arrowshafts.

Fig. 146. Cutting the tip end below the joint.

The twining process is continued until the required length is achieved. Splicing new length to the cord is done by carefully laying the new sinew alongside the last inch of the old strand and twisting the two together. If the ends are carefully tapered for splicing with a sharp-edged tool, the diameter of the cord will not be increased (Figs. 140–144).

A sinew string is finished by stretching it between two points and rubbing saliva into it until all the rough spots are smoothed down. It must then dry in this position.

Arrows

Several different kinds of serviceable arrowshafts can be constructed. Since feathers are often at a premium in the wilderness, arrows are often made without them. And when feathers are available, glue for fletching them is sometimes not. Because of these limitations, methods of arrow production in primitive situations are vastly different from those ordinarily used. As a result, the end products differ in many ways.

Arrows without fletchings are made from light woods and reeds. The common river reed (*Phragmites communis*) is best for such arrows. But willow (*Salix*) and a variety of light pithy woods can be used when reeds are not available (Fig. 145).

Reeds suitable for arrows are cut when dry. The length of each shaft should be about twenty-four inches, and the cuts should be made

Fig. 147. Straightening the reed shaft.

one-half inch above a joint on what will be the nock end and three or four inches below a joint on what will be the tip end (Figs. 146, 148). This allows a strong place for the nock to be cut and leaves a hollow tube at the other end to receive a foreshaft. A reed shaft is straightened by rubbing grease (if available) on its joints and holding it over hot coals or on a hot rock until it is heated and then lightly bending it until it is straight, or as straight as one can make it (Fig. 147). It must be held in this position until cool. Reed stems are difficult to straighten between the joints, and one must be careful not to break them during the straightening process. Pitch is applied and sinew is wrapped around the tip end of the shaft to keep it from splitting. The nock is cut at the tip and wrapped with sinew for added strength (Fig. 148).

Foreshafts are cut from any heavy hardwood tree or bush in six- to eight-inch lengths. One end is sharpened to a point and hardened in a fire, and the other end is blunted and inserted into the hollow end of the reed stem. The arrow is then complete (Fig. 149).

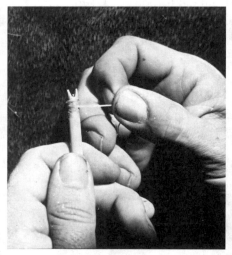

Fig. 148. Wrapping the nock end.

Fig. 149. Completed arrow.

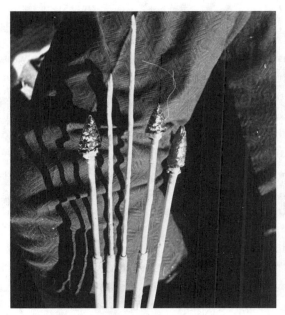

Fig. 150. Reed arrows with stone-tipped foreshafts.

These flimsy arrows are best used with a lightweight bow and are effective for flock shooting and small game. A dozen or more can be made in one evening around the fire. They may last for only a few shots, but the simplicity and speed with which they are constructed makes them important and effective arrows. These same reed shafts can be made more accurate and deadly by adding stone points and fletchings (Fig. 150).

Native woods best suited for sturdy hunting arrows are chokecherry (*Prunus*), serviceberry (*Amelanchier*), rose (*Rosa*), currant (*Ribes*), and willow (*Salix*). The shafts are selected from young shoots found in shaded areas where they must grow tall and straight to reach the sunlight. After they are cut, they must be dried in the sun for one day. The bark is then peeled and the still-green shafts are cut into lengths several inches longer than the size of the finished arrows. Next, the shafts are sorted according to size and weight, tied into bundles of five or six, and left to dry slowly in the shade for two days. The drying process can be speeded up by placing the shafts in sunlight or holding them over hot coals, but the danger of splitting is increased when quick drying is used. However, effective arrowshafts can be turned out within a few hours after they are cut if they are dried with heat. It is very important that the shafts be completely dry before they are made into arrows. If they are made in groups of five, completing each step with all five arrows before going on, much time is saved and the arrows are better matched for more accurate shooting.

Straightening wood shafts is simple and is done in the same manner as described for reed shafts. All one has to do is heat the crooked part and work it over the knee or with the fingers. An arrow wrench, which is a flat bone with a hole drilled in it, is also effective for prying out crooks (Fig. 151). But one can get the job done much faster by gripping the shaft with the teeth just below the crook and then wrenching it straight with the hands (Fig. 152).

When the shafts are completely straight and dry, they are scraped down and smoothed with a chip of stone or broken glass (Fig. 153). Scraped lengthwise, the shafts become round and even. If a stone tip is to be used, the nock for the bowstring should be at the large end of the shaft. If the point is going to be simply sharpened and hardened in the fire, the nock should be made in the small end. Nocking the shaft for the bowstring is done by sawing the shaft with a sharp chip of stone (Fig. 154). The nock should be U-shaped and about one-fourth inch deep.

Fig. 151. Prying out crooks with an arrow wrench.

Fig. 152. Straightening an arrowshaft.

Fig. 153. Smoothing the arrowshaft.

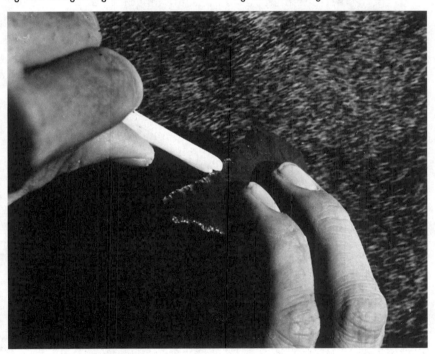

Fig. 154. Nocking the shaft with a stone chip.

Fletching an arrow by hand is not difficult if one uses glue. The feathers are bound in place until the glue dries and then the ends of the feathers are secured with sinew. Animal glue, by far the most effective, is made by boiling down skins, hooves, or fish skins. Pine pitch and some plant saps, though sticky, do not make good glues for fletching.

Since animal glue is difficult to make, fletching without glue is often necessary in the wilderness. To accomplish this, one selects long feathers from the same bird wing or from the same side of the bird's tail. They are split down the center of the quill with a fine chip of obsidian or other sharp stone. Then the arrowmaker sits on the ground and holds one end of the feather on a smooth rock with his big toe, and stretching the feather taut with his left hand, scrapes away the excess spine with a sharp stone chip (Fig. 155). A little practice enables the arrowmaker to prepare feathers with professional accuracy.

All the feathers are then cut to the same length, four to six inches, and one inch of the web is stripped off at the base. The feathers are attached to the shaft as follows:

- First, measure the point on the shaft that the web of the feather will reach when fully fletched.

- Then measure up the shaft toward the nock about one inch, the distance from the stripped quill to the beginning of the web.

- Place one feather on the shaft upside down and invert it so that the tip of its base is even with the one-inch mark on the shaft.

- Bind the stripped end of the feather to the shaft in this position, using only one or two wraps of sinew.

- Then place the other two feathers in the same position as the first, and bind all of them down tightly with sinew, again using only one or two wrappings.

- Lift each feather, bending the quill at the point where the web starts, and lay it flat against the shaft. Do not strip the tips on the top end of the feathers, but lightly ruffle them back and dampen them with the fingers to hold them out of the way.

- Wrap sinew over the ends of the feathers just below the nock, leaving enough feather tip sticking out to grasp with the fingers.

Fig. 155. Scraping away the excess spine.   Fig. 156. Measuring the web position.

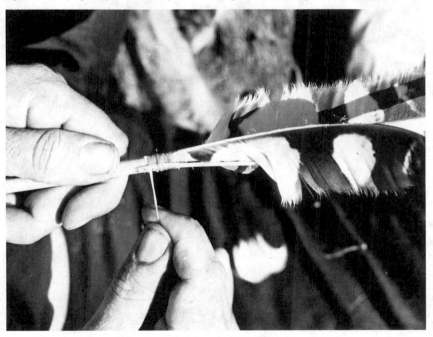

Fig. 157. Binding feathers to the shaft in the inverted position.

- Grasping each tip with the fingers or with an improvised pair of pinchers, pull them tight, flattening the quill against the shaft and stiffening the vane.

- Finally, wrap on additional sinew to secure the feathers tightly, allow the sinew to dry, and trim off the excess with a stone chip (Figs. 156–162).

A simpler method of fletching calls for smearing a small amount of hot pine pitch on the shaft where the ends of the feathers will be located and also just below the nock where the tip ends of the feathers will be bound. The pitch keeps the fletchings from pulling loose. The feathers are then pressed firmly into the warm pitch and wrapped with

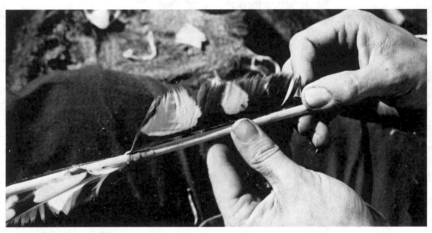

Fig. 158. Bending and laying feathers flat against the shaft.

Fig. 159. Wrapping the ends of the feathers.

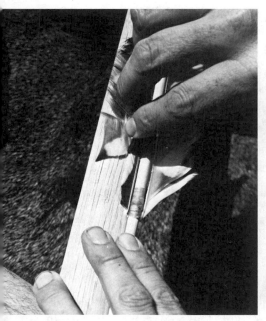

Fig. 160. Trimming the excess feathers.

Fig. 161. Pressing the feathers into the pitch.

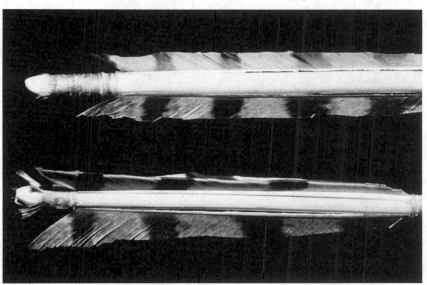

Fig. 162. Both methods of fletching.

sinew. Next the tip ends of the fletching are bound down and pulled to flatten the quill against the shaft (Figs. 161, 162).

When the arrowmaker begins the process of attaching points, he discovers that filing a notch to receive a stone or bone point is hard work without a steel knife. It is much easier to break out a notch by using the following trick:

- Cut a notch on each side of the shaft at the point where it will end. This should present no problem because the shaft was previously cut several inches longer than necessary.

- Cut another notch on each side of the shaft between the first two notches and one-fourth inch above them.

- The excess shaft then breaks off when submitted to gentle pressure and bending, and a deep notch is left in the end to receive the head (Fig. 163).

Before fitting the point to the shaft, the notch should be smoothed and sanded to fit the contour of the point. The point is then inserted in the notch, wrapped with sinew, and, if possible, glued with pitch. When the sinew is dry, the arrow is complete and ready for use (Fig. 164).

Constructing Atlatls and Spears

A simple but effective weapon for large game is the atlatl. This device predates the bow and arrow and was used by ancient peoples to hunt large game. The Australian aborigines, the Eskimos, and some Mexican Indians still use it.

The atlatl is a stick used to throw a light spear or dart with greater force and distance than is possible with the arm alone. It acts as an extension of the arm, thus giving greater power to the thrower. The atlatl is about two feet long, two inches wide, and one-half inch thick. A prong is carved at one end to fit into the hollow butt of the spear, and two loops are tied at the other end, through which the thrower's fingers pass (Fig. 165).

The spear or dart is five or six feet long with a foreshaft of hardwood about six inches long, tipped with a stone point. The butt end is hollowed to receive the prong of the atlatl, and two feathers are tied to the sides near the butt end to help balance the spear in flight. The spear shaft may be made of reed grass or any straight shoot. A young straight juniper shoot is excellent but rarely found. Pine saplings growing in

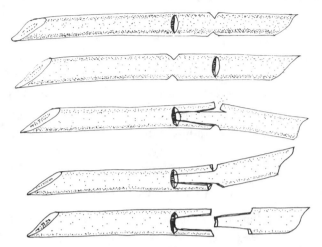

Fig. 163. Breaking out a notch.

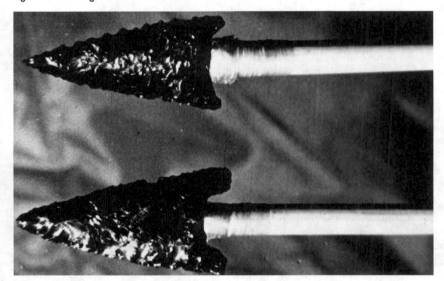

Fig. 164. Stone-tipped arrows.

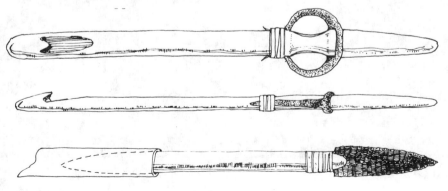

Fig. 165. Atlatl——throwing board and details of the spear foreshaft.

dense thickets are sometimes straight and slender, but any shaft can be straightened by heating and bending.

A hole is drilled in the tip end to receive the foreshaft, and cord is wrapped around the drilled end to keep it from splitting on impact. The feathering of the shaft need not be elaborate; two feathers tied securely with sinew at both ends and in the middle will do. The finished spear should be slender and not too heavy or cumbersome (Fig. 166).

The following suggestions will aid in constructing the atlatl and spear:

- A natural bump or twig may be utilized for the prong on the atlatl.

- The wood is carved and shaped with stone tools in the same manner as arrows are made.

- Drilling a foreshaft socket is best done with a stone or bone drill set in the ground or held between the feet. The shaft is then twirled on it by being spun between the palms of the hands (Fig. 167).

Using the atlatl with skill demands much practice, and for this, blunt spears without foreshafts should be used. They are also good for hunt-

Fig. 166. Finished spear.

Fig. 167. Drilling a shaft by spinning it.

Fig. 168. Correct position for throwing the spear or dart.

Fig. 169. Throwing the spear or dart.

ing small game. A snapping, powerful throw is not necessary. Rather, the spear should be thrown overhand with an even sweeping motion straight at the target, not lobbed over to it. When the butt end of the spear tends to dip down, spoiling its flight, this is a sign that the thrower is flipping it too hard or that the spear is too heavy (Figs. 168, 169).

Making Cordage

Strange as it may seem, a piece of string can become the most important item in a survival situation, for it is required in the construction of nearly everything. Equally surprising is the simplicity with which it can be manufactured in nature. Anything from sewing thread to rope can be made from a number of common plants.

Materials

Listed here are commonly found fibers and their uses:

- Stinging Nettle (*Urtica*, colorplate 20). The stalks of this plant contain a very strong fiber that can be used to make thread, fish line, string, yarn, snares, nets, ropes, cloth, bowstrings, sandals, blankets, and woven sacks. The fiber is obtained by pounding dry stems to remove the woody parts, then cleaning the remaining fiber by hand.

- Milkweed (*Asclepias*, colorplate 16). The stalks of this plant contain a silky fiber that can be used when the plant is green or dry. Best when harvested dry, it is processed in the same way as nettle and can serve the same purposes.

- Dogbane (*Apocynum cannabinum*, colorplate 9). This is perhaps the best fiber plant found in the West. The stalks contain a fine, soft, silky fiber that is easily worked. It is processed and used the same as nettle and milkweed.

- Haw, Hawthorn, or Thornapple (*Crataegus*). The inner white bark of this tree makes good cordage. Though it cannot be used for as many different products as the plants just listed, it can be stripped and twisted into string and rope and will serve in a pinch for fish line, snares, and sandals. The bark is strongest when wet and becomes a little stiff when dry. Other trees with similar bark that is good for cordage are willow, elm, spruce (roots), rose, and snowberry.

- Sagebrush (*Artemisia tridentata*, colorplate 26). This plant has dry bark that can be stripped from the trunk and twisted into cordage.

Though this bark is not strong, it has a wide variety of uses. It can be made into coarse woven bags and blankets and is the principal cordage for making sandals. The rope made from it is not very strong but will serve for tying things together and for holding timbers in position for shelters. It may also be pounded and used for tinder. Other plants with similar bark are juniper (*Juniperus*) and cliffrose (*Cowania*). The barks of all these plants can be gathered in large quantities and used for bedding and thatching material.

Twisting

After collecting the materials, the more involved part of making cordage begins. Listed here are the steps involved in twisting fibers by hand. They are essentially the same as those given in the section on making bowstring:

- Two strips of fiber are selected and held in the left hand between the thumb and forefinger.
- The fiber farthest from the body is grasped in the fingers of the right hand and twisted clockwise a few turns.
- The twisted strand is then laid counterclockwise over the remaining strand and becomes the one closest to the body.
- The second strand, now farthest from the body, is twisted a few turns and laid over the first strand exactly as before. This is continued until the ends of the strands are reached.
- New lengths of fiber are spliced on at this point. This is done by twisting the last two inches of the ends onto the new fibers and continuing the process of twisting and folding. It is best to alternate the lengths of the strands so that the splices do not appear at the same place in the finished string.
- When short lengths of string are needed for tying something or sewing a few stitches, there is a quick way to produce them. Simply hold one end of a long strand in the left hand and roll it in one direction on the thigh with the right hand. When the strand is rolled tight, grasp one end in each hand and place the middle between the teeth. Now put the two ends together and hold them tightly. Drop the end held by the teeth and the string will twine together automatically from the tension produced when it was twisted and rolled on the

thigh. This results in a two-ply cord that is half the length of the original strand.

Preparing Sinew

The long tendons from the legs of animals and the even longer ones from their backs can be prepared and fashioned into cordage that is unequaled in strength. The best bowstrings are made from sinew (see Bowstrings, above). The simple strands also serve to haft arrowpoints and other tools to their wooden shafts. They are wrapped on while wet and do not need to be tied, since the sinew is sticky enough to serve as its own glue.

When the tendons are taken from the animal, they should be cleaned and placed in the sun until they are completely hard and dry and then placed on a smooth rock and pounded with another rock until they are soft, fluffy, and white. The sinew will then strip apart into fine threads. It can be used dry for sewing thread, twisted into cords, or moistened for wrapping and hafting stone implements (Fig. 170).

Weaving Clothes and Other Items

Like anything else that is worthwhile, weaving takes time. But a number of useful items can be made with the simple plain weave, an over-and-under technique. Cattail and bulrush stems produce good mats for floor coverings, beds, and shelter covers.

The twining method is used for making blankets, bags, sandals, fish traps, and some baskets. The foundation strands are called the warp and the interwoven strands are called the weft. There are two weft strands in twining, one going over the warp and one going under it, and they are crossed between each warp.

Most baskets used for water bottles and for carrying and harvesting seeds are made with the coiled technique. A basket is built up from the base with a growing spiral consisting of two small withes of willow and a bundle of fibrous material, usually grass or bark. Each coil is then stitched to the one below with a thin splint of cambium-layer squaw bush or willow. The splint is passed through the coil with the aid of a bone awl (Fig. 171).

The following tips will save time and make the weaver's work more efficient:

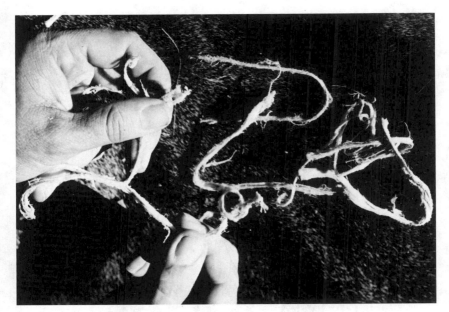

Fig. 170. Prepared sinew.

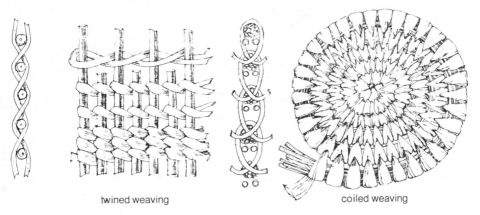

twined weaving   coiled weaving

Fig. 171. Two major types of weaving.

Fig. 172. Blanket woven from bark.

- Grasses and reeds selected for weaving should be dry, not green.

- The dried material should be soaked in water just before it is used and kept pliable during the weaving process.

- Willow weaving materials should be cut when green, split twice to the cambium layer, left to dry, and soaked in water just before they are used.

- The leftover inside core of splints is used for the foundation rods and the outside or sapwood used for the splints. Other materials such as flat bark strips and rush strips can also be used for splints.

Large burden sacks, packs, blankets, storage-pit liners, clothing, and sandals can be made from the soft inner bark of the sagebrush and cliffrose plants. The strips of bark are fluffed and slightly twisted for the warp strands. Cords and flat strips are used for the weft. A loose twined weave is sufficient for the burden sacks and packs. Sandals are easily made from the bark in a few hours. Time does not usually permit refinement of the sandals, but serviceable ones can be twined in about

Fig. 173. Size of woven blanket.

Fig. 174. Twined basket made from bulrush.

Fig. 175. Sandals woven from bark.

three hours and will last through about three days of moderate use (Figs. 172–175).

Woven water jugs are merely coiled baskets with small openings at the top. They are lined with pitch that is smeared on the inside before the constricting top is made. The remainder is then lined in this way: a lump of pitch is placed inside the basket with a hot rock and the container is shaken until the pitch has melted and spread over the interior surface. Pine pitch is prepared by boiling lumps of it for fifteen minutes or so and then skimming the surface with a flat stick. It must then be heated before use. Another method consists of burning the pitch on a sloping rock. The turpentine burns away, and the pure pitch runs down the rock to where it can be collected and molded into small balls.

Baskets can be made watertight without the pitch liner if they are constructed with a very tight coiled weave. The advantage of this is that one can boil water in them merely by placing hot stones into the bas-

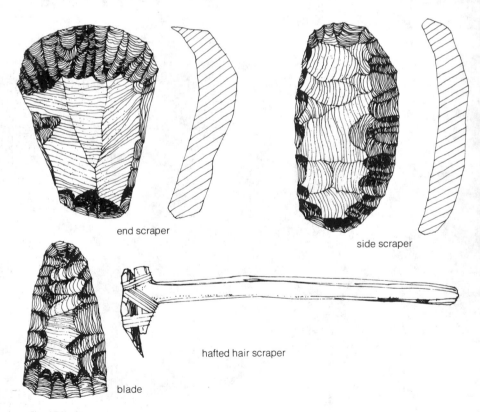

end scraper

side scraper

hafted hair scraper

blade

Fig. 176. Stone scrapers.

kets. This is called stone boiling. Stone boiling can be done in a skin or paunch instead of a woven basket as well.

Making Rawhide

Making good rawhide requires a little more care than just letting a green hide dry until it is stiff. The following steps must be taken to render it usable for moccasin soles, bags, pails, ropes, boxes, and other utilitarian items:

- The hide must be soaked in water a day or more if it has previously been dried out, but if it is green, this step is not necessary.

- The hide is staked out with the flesh side up, and all the fat and excess tissue is scraped off with a flesher, which is made from a long bone of a large animal. One side is honed down to a very sharp edge and small teeth are cut in it. Then a strap is fastened to the top to serve as a wrist support. This implement is used to hack, peel, and scrape the fat from the hide. Stone scrapers are held in the hand and applied in a drawing motion across the hide (Fig. 176, 177).

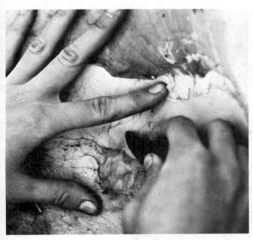

Fig. 177. Scraping off fat and excess tissue.

Fig. 178. Hide staked for scraping.

■ The hide is washed clean and left staked out for a couple of days to dry in the sun (Fig. 178). During the washing process, the scrapers should be used to make sure that all fat is removed. Water is normally used for washing, but better results can be achieved by using urine. This may be repulsive to some people, but it stands proven as a superior way to clean a hide. The urine should soak into the hide until

Fig. 179. Frame stretching.

the fat is completely dissolved by the strong acids. The urine is then scraped off, along with the dissolved fat. The urine cleaning is followed with a good washing of water.

- The hide is dried until it is stiff. Then remove the stakes, turn it over, and restake it. All the hair is now removed with a hair scraper. A sideways motion is used and every inch of the hide is covered. This backbreaking work is made somewhat easier if the hide is first soaked in a solution of water and wood ashes overnight. This loosens the hair so that it slips out rather than being shaved off by the hair scraper. Hair scrapers are simply small hoes made of wood, bone, or horn with a sharp stone blade attached to the hoe end. The blade must be sharpened often (Fig. 176).

- The final step in making rawhide is to place the dry hide on a soft pad of grass or old blankets and pound it with a blunt stone hammer weighing three or four pounds. The hide should be struck with short glancing blows, and every inch of it must be covered if the grain is to be broken and the hide is to become white and soft. Rawhide prepared this way is just as tough as tanned shoe leather and almost as soft.

Tools Required for Tanning Skins

Tanning skins in the wild requires special tools. Circumstances in a primitive setting often limit the availability of certain resources, so some of the tools listed here have alternates that, though often more difficult to use, will serve the purpose. Also, slightly different methods are adaptable to different locales and lifestyles. Once mastered, all will produce the same results.

Stretching Tools

Skins must be stretched several times during the tanning process. There are two basic methods:

- Frame stretching requires sturdy poles, lashings, and about one hundred feet of small-diameter rope or lacing. The frame poles are set up (Fig. 179) with lashings and braces so that the inside dimensions are approximately one foot larger than the hide to be tanned. The lacing rope may be baling twine, rawhide cord, yucca strips, or dried and twisted cattail leaves. A long cord will enable continuous lacing, while natural plant cordage requires short strips tied onto the frame separately.

- Ground stretching makes the graining process in tanning more difficult and requires the tanner to work in a stooped or kneeling position. However, the actual stretching process is much simpler, requiring only a smooth ground surface and wooden stakes. The stakes are made from hardwood shoots about three-quarters of an inch in diameter and twelve to fourteen inches long. Each stake should have a piece of cord wrapped tightly around its top end to prevent it from splitting while being pounded into the ground.

Scrapers

Fleshing tools can be made of steel, bone, or stone. Steel stays sharp longer but is no better than bone or stone for doing the job. Stone hand scrapers are easiest to make but are more difficult to use because they tire the arms. (See Working Stone, earlier in this chapter).

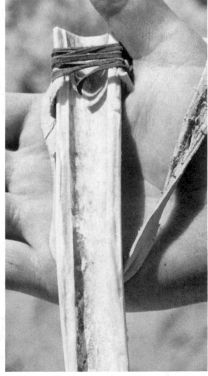

Fig. 180. Bone fleshing tool.   Fig. 181. Bone fleshing tool with toothed edge.

The long bone scrapers with a wrist strap work better and they are relatively easy to make and sharpen (Fig. 180). Long leg bones of deer, elk, cow, horse, or other large animal are split and honed down by rubbing on a sanding stone. The chisel-shaped cutting edge is then serrated to produce jagged gripping tines. A strap is tied onto the top end of the scraper and looped to form a wrist brace (Fig. 181).

Hafted stone or steel blades make excellent scrapers and may be made in a variety of shapes and sizes (Figs. 182, 183). Hafting increases power and pressure for scraping hides. Tools for tanning should be made easy to disassemble for sharpening and blade replacement. This is accomplished by wrapping with buckskin, cordage, or string rather than with

Fig. 182. Hafted stone scraper.

sinew and pitch. Knots should be easy to undo. Bone handles are especially suited to socket and wedge hafting, when a stone blade is fitted into the socket and wedged there. Hoe-shaped scrapers should be large and heavy for best results.

Hair Scrapers

Removing hair from hides requires a fine cutting edge, and steel or stone are the only scrapers that work well. Bone- or antler-handled hafted scrapers are good, and the hoe-shaped heavy ones are best. Be sure the blades are razor sharp. Stone blades are best made using sharp blanks with edges that are not retouched (Fig. 176). See Working Stone, earlier in this chapter, for details on making blades.

Graining Tools

Two types of rubbing and graining tools are needed for preparing hides. The first has a sharp or wedge-shaped blade, which may be made of wood (Fig. 184). Some of the hide scrapers listed above will also serve

Fig. 183. Stone graining tool.

Fig. 184. Hafted stone scraper.

Fig. 185. Blunt wooden graining tool.

as blade graining tools. The second tool needed is a heavy pole or stick with a blunt rounded edge (Fig. 185). This tool must be smooth and without any sharp edges. It is used with greater pressure in the graining process.

Rubbing and Sanding Stones

Tanning stones are handheld and shaped like a flattened loaf. They should be smooth and free of irregular edges. They are used to rub on the brains in the tanning process.

Sanding stones may be any rough pieces of pumice or sandstone that will act like sandpaper in rubbing off hard-to-clean areas and in sanding off rough areas on the surface of the skin (Fig. 186).

Fig. 186. Rubbing stone.

Fig. 187. Mouse skin finger mitten.

Skinning and Care of Hides

Any animal skin can be made useful, tanned or untanned. At least one of my students kept enough pelts from his trapline to fashion some finger mittens of untanned mouse skins (Fig. 187).

Skinning

Depending on what you want to do with them, pelts may be cased or split. Casing a hide means pulling the entire skin off the carcass from the rear forward, with cuts made only around the feet of the animal and from the back legs to the tail. This method allows the skin to be made into mittens, bags, quivers, and other holding utensils. It is the standard method of pelting most animals for the fur market. Splitting a skin involves the same procedures as casing, but the hide is split up the legs and all the way up the belly to the chin, and the hide is laid out flat.

Raw or Green Skins

At the very least, a hide may be dried and used as a stiff bag or laid out flat as bedding. Green hides are warm and can be formed into stiff, body-hugging quilts in an emergency.

On one occasion with a group of survival trainees, I butchered a large buck sheep (it lasted only one meal) and we threw the hide over a limb. Later that evening, because of the "sardine" conditions, I relinquished my sleeping spot in our small cave. I pulled that green, wet hide off the tree and, with a little help from one of the guys, wrapped up tightly with the wool side in. My knees were tucked up, my feet just fit inside, and my head was covered. Neatly wrapped and tucked in, I spent the night just outside the cave. Toward morning it snowed, then cleared off, and the temperature dropped near zero. I needed help getting out of my solid cocoon, which was frozen stiff, but it was toasty warm inside.

Green hides can be dried for keeping by laying or hanging them out in the open air and sunlight. No parts should be allowed to overlap or be folded, as flies and moisture will spoil the skin quickly. Dried skins should be given a preliminary scraping to remove the major pieces of flesh and fat that might spoil and damage the skin. Thin layers of flesh will dry along with the hide and will not need removal until the tanning process is begun. Dried skins will keep a long time. However, salted hides do not brain-tan as well.

Uses for Animal Hides

A skin's uses in a primitive setting are limited only by the imagination. Listed below are a few ideas that have been tested in survival and primitive-living camps:

- Deer, elk, moose, antelope, horse, calf, cow, goat; leather and rawhide with the hair removed: best used for clothing, footgear, straps, snowshoes, quivers, bags, string, rope, hinges, bowstrings, snare lines, sewing laces, boxes, pack sacks and frames, hafting wrap, and so on. **Note:** Hides of hollow-haired animals such as deer, elk, and antelope do not tan well with the hair left on, and they shed badly.

- Horse, cow, calf, sheep, mountain goat, bear, cougar, bobcat, wolf, marten, coyote, weasel, mink, beaver, otter, raccoon, skunk; leather and rawhide with the hair left on: best used for robes, bedding, clothing, bags, quivers, hats, cold-weather footgear, and so on. Badger is noted as a tough hide for moccasin soles, but its value as a fur makes it uneconomical for this use except in emergencies.

- Rabbit, muskrat, rockchuck, pack rat, mice, and other small rodents; leather and rawhide with the hair left on: bags, string, hats, mittens, fur liners for footgear, clothing, ponchos, and blankets made of twisted fur strips.

- Birds skinned with feathers intact and dried, lightly tanned: sew inside clothing for extra warmth; sew breast skins together for warm robes or ponchos; use feathers and down plucked from skins as insulation; may be twisted into warm feather-cord blankets.

- Snakes, lizards, and other reptiles; leather and rawhide: small pouches, wrappings for handles, small sealers and wraps for moisture protection, and so on.

The Tanning Process

With tools in hand and information well in mind, tanning may be a swift process taking from six to ten actual working hours, the curing time spreading the whole project over two or three days. Skins vary in thickness. Each skin has its own qualities, which must be dealt with in order to produce leather or soft furs. In the steps given below, a deerskin is the example. The procedure is the same for all skins tanned with the hair removed. Furs and hides tanned with the hair on require more gentle handling, and, of course, the hair is not removed.

Soaking

Dry skins must be soaked in water until thoroughly soft. A fresh green hide need not be soaked if it is to be stretched right away. Soaking may be done by sinking the hide in a ditch or stream or by tying it to the bank with a rope and letting it drag in fast-running water. Some tanners will let a skin drag in cold swift water for a week, or until the hair has all been slipped and forced off by the water pressure. To do this, tie the anchor rope near the tail so that the current will run against the hair grain. The epidermis is more easily scraped off after the hair is gone. However, the time involved makes this step impractical in a survival situation.

Most skins can be softened overnight by soaking them in a container of cool water. If a skin is left in longer than twelve hours, check it often and change the water if it gets scummy. Upon removing the skin from the water, scrub it to help remove blood and debris.

Fig. 188. Stretching on a frame.

Stretching

A fresh green or soaked hide must be stretched immediately and pulled tight with the flesh side up. If the hide is stretched on a frame, begin with the head and lace the cord loosely around the frame and through small holes punched in the edges of the hide about three inches apart. As you progress around the frame, begin pulling the lacing tight until the whole skin is taut. If you are using short pieces of cord, as with cordage made from plant fiber, pull the cords tight from opposite sides and work back and forth until an even stretch is achieved. This takes about an hour (Fig. 188).

Ground stretching is less difficult but makes scraping harder. Perfectly level ground is a must. The hide is spread out with the flesh side up and a stake is driven through a hole punched at the head. Then drive a stake at the tail, pulling the hide tight. Go back and forth to opposite ends, driving stakes about every three to five inches and pulling the skin tight with each stake. The holes in the skin can be punched with a large bone awl or knife before each stake is driven. Driving stakes is easier if a steel stake is used to punch a hole in the ground and then removed and the wooden one pounded in. This saves wooden stakes from being beaten down or broken if they hit a rock (Fig. 189).

Fig. 189. Stretching on ground.

Fleshing

Whether you use steel, stone, or bone tools, the process of fleshing a hide is the same. If you are using bone or hafted stone scrapers, work while the hide is wet, scraping and hacking off all the flesh, membrane, and fat adhering to it. If only hand scrapers of stone are available, it may work better to let the hide dry first. Then scrape hard, pulling the membrane off in sheets. One benefit of dry scraping is that you salvage the membrane sheets, which can be cut into strips and used in the same way as sinew for hafting.

Scraping begins at the head and progresses down to the tail. Be careful not to make holes in the more tender parts of the belly, flank, and tail area. Scrub and wash bloody areas as you scrape. Soapy water made with nondetergent soap flakes or crushed yucca root helps this process if available. Restretch the hide if it loosens, and let it dry after it is scraped.

Dehairing

Turn the dry skin over with the hair side up. Two things come off the hide in dehairing—the hair and the epidermis, or first layer of skin. The hide will not remain soft if the epidermis is left on. The best scraper for dehairing is the heavy, hoe-shaped one, with a steel or stone blade. Bone-bladed scrapers will not work. The prime factor is the sharpness of the blade. The blades will need sharpening frequently. Stone-bladed scrapers are best without retouched edges, which require switching blades every few minutes, but retouching will work if done carefully so that no jagged edges remain on the blade. See Working Stone, earlier in this chapter, for details on retouching or pressure-flaking stone blades.

With careful, even strokes, beginning at the head, scrape off the hair and epidermis, working down the hide toward the tail. It will be impossible to get the hair off around the edges close to the lacings or stakes. Leave these parts alone and remove the hair when the hide is cut from the frame or stakes.

Braining

The agent that breaks down the glue or glycerin and loosens the fibers of the skin is found in the brains of animals. Generally, a moose brain is sufficient in quantity to tan a moose hide, a mouse brain is sufficient to tan a mouse skin, and so forth. However, any brain will do for any kind of skin if the quantity is sufficient.

Fig. 190. Cooked brains.

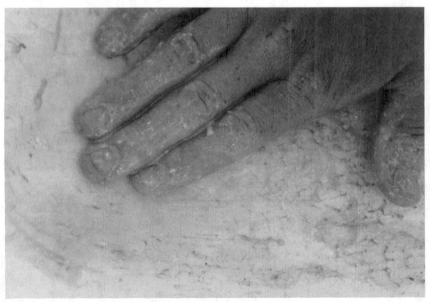

Fig. 191. Rubbing on the brain tanning solution.

There are many recipes for preserving brains until the skin is ready for tanning. A few of these are as follows:

■ Heat the brains in a little water, and while they are heating mash and squeeze them between the fingers, pulling at the fibrous membranes until the mixture is too hot to keep your hands in. Then spread the thin oily mixture on a smooth board and lay it out to dry. It will keep several days in a cool place. When ready to use it, peel it off the board and reconstitute it in water, again cooking it slightly.

■ Mix the heated brains with the moss found hanging from pine trees, form into small cakes, and dry. The moss acts as a binder and can be removed from the mixture when it is reconstituted.

■ Cook the brains until they are yellow and mix with the spinal cord; put the mixture into an intestine casing as if you were making sausage, and seal the ends. This will keep in a cool place for several days. To reconstitute, cook in a little water until hot to the touch.

The delicate brain mix is always cooked lightly to increase its keeping quality. Raw brains, if left out, will spoil and smell bad in just a few hours. Fresh brains are preferred over any of the above, and if obtained at the right time or kept frozen, will do a better job. Just cook, mash, and apply (Figs. 190, 191).

There are other tanning agents that, though often easier to work with, are not as good nor as available in a wilderness setting. Applied just like the brains, egg whites, nondetergent soap flakes, or even lard will cause a bacterial breakdown of the glue and glycerin in a skin.

When the brains are ready for use, there should be a thick soupy mixture surrounded by a thin broth or liquid in the container. Smear the thick paste on the skin starting with the flesh side, and then put what is left on the hair side of a dehaired skin. Use your warm hands and heated tanning stones to rub the mixture in. Then, with a brush or rag, brush on the broth that is left in the container. This will thin the paste and cause the brains to soak in better. Let the mixture absorb into the skin for six hours or more before going on to the next step.

Graining

The skin should be quite damp and somewhat pliable with the brains on. Also, its thickness will have increased. For a dehaired skin, unstake or unlace and again soak the skin in water, submerging it overnight. Skins with the hair left on should not be soaked, but dampen them by applying warm water on the flesh side. Warm, wet rags speed up the process.

If you are soaking the skin in a container, add some pounded yucca root or biscuit-root or nondetergent soap flakes to the water if available, and suds it up. This helps clean the pores and removes the animal smell from the hide.

The next day, remove the hide from the water. If a stretcher was used, restretch the skin on the frame and use the wedge-shaped graining tool to squeeze the water from the hide. Apply pressure over every inch and scrape and stretch the fibers until most of the water has oozed out. Then, with the blunt graining pole, go over the entire hide again, stretching and rubbing until the skin is nearly dry but still slightly damp and cool to the touch. This may take an hour, though sunlight will speed up the drying process. The secret to tanning is in how well you keep the fibers in the hide stretched while it is drying.

Next cut the skin from the frame around the perimeter, leaving only the lacing holes and hair that could not be removed before. If time will not permit the final step of rubbing, roll the skin up and store it in a plastic bag or slightly damp cloth.

If the hide has been staked to the ground during the tanning process, then a little different procedure is needed for graining, since the stretching frame is not available. Trim off the rough edges of the skin and wring it out by twisting it on a stick. Then bind the blade graining tool to an upright post about four and one-half feet above the ground and pull the skin back and forth across it, covering every inch of both sides for a dehaired skin. Then do the same with the blunt graining pole. This will produce the desired effect, but it is more difficult for the operator. Repeat until the skin is cool and only slightly damp to the touch.

Rubbing

The final step in tanning, and a crucial one for producing soft, high-quality skins, is the high-friction rubbing needed to create a little heat and finish the drying, stretching, and breaking of the grain. A number of methods can be used, depending on what tools are available.

If you have a long rope about half an inch in diameter, loop and tie it around a tree trunk about seven feet from the ground. Bring the long

Fig. 192. Women in buckskins.

end of the rope down and loop and tie it around the trunk a foot or so from the ground so that the vertical length of rope between the two loops is taut. Place the hide smoothly behind the vertical length of rope and begin pulling it hard against the rope. The skin will stretch noticeably. Grasp the skin at different points all around its perimeter and pull, pull, pull. When the skin is fully stretched, begin the friction process by pulling the hide back and forth in a seesaw motion over the rope. Rub it all around the perimeter and from every angle until the entire hide is completely dry. The final product will be white and soft.

If a rope is not available, stretch the skin by sitting on the ground and hooking the skin over your feet. Then pull against your feet from every angle. When the skin has been stretched, it can be rubbed by pulling it over a slender, smooth sapling. A better rubbing method is to make a pole blade with one beveled edge and secure it between two posts. Pull the skin back and forth over the blade to stretch and dry it.

When the skin is completely dry, it may be finished with sanding stones. Any area of the skin that is blemished, rough, or spotty can be sanded to produce a fluffy texture overall.

At this point the tanning is essentially finished. The leather is white and ready to use for clothing or any other purpose (Fig. 192).

Smoking Skins

When a white-tanned skin gets wet, it will often dry stiff and need reworking to restore the softness. Smoking the hide will help prevent this and also give the skin a buckskin-brown color and pleasant wood-smoke aroma.

Sew up the skin into a large bag or tube with the tail and head ends left open. Attach the head end to a crosspole and stake the base down over a small firepit from six to ten inches deep and filled with glowing-hot coals. Leave a small opening at the base of the tube through which you can drop some punk or wet or green wood chips onto the hot coals. Sage or willow are good woods for smoking, though any wood will work. The object is to get the chips to smoke, not burn. Careful watching and a handful of dirt kept ready are necessary to prevent flames from ruining the hide. It only takes a few minutes to brown the skin. The longer it is left, the deeper the color becomes. Smoke one or both sides as desired. After smoking, roll up the hide and put it away in a bag for a day. This lets the smoke be absorbed. The aroma of smoked leather will remain as long as the leather lasts.

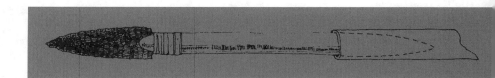

The hand drill.

The Last Great Lesson

After all is read and said and practiced and a feeling of "making it" prevails, there remains still the final value of this little book. For it has, indeed, saved at least two lives in the wilderness, according to a small newspaper article I noticed while traveling through Utah. It was titled, "Survival Book Saves Lives of Two Youth."

The article told a harrowing story of two teenage boys on a backpacking expedition in the Wasatch Mountains. They had packed for fair weather, with food and necessities. But as nature designed it, things changed quickly. They became lost and hiked deeper into the mountains. Along the way, crucial parts of their camping gear became lost or was discarded. The final blow came in the form of an early snowstorm that dumped fourteen inches in just a few hours.

The boys finally gave up trying to hike out. They decided to camp and wait for rescue. Making camp in blowing snow was difficult and the shelter they put up barely broke the wind. They needed a good fire and a supply of wood. The wood supply proved to be plentiful, so they stacked a bunch of it and settled into making a fire. They had only a few matches and after four or five tries they realized there was no dry tinder close by. One of the boys remembered he had a book called *Outdoor Survival*

Skills included in his pack. He fished it out, turned to the chapter on fire, and read it thoroughly in the fading light of day. He turned to his partner and said, "Now I know how to get this fire going." The boy began tearing pages from the book and stuffing them in with the kindling. With their last two matches they lit the pages and started the fire that saved their lives that night!

Colorplates of Useful Plants

The following colorplates identify ninety-six different plants that can be used to fulfill a variety of outdor needs. The pictures are arranged alphabetically by common name. Appearing below the common name(s) are the scientific—genus and species—names, in italic. The different uses of the plant—as food, medicine, tinder, fiber—are listed last.

These pictures are keyed by colorplate number to the plants described in Chapter 5. When several species of a genus are useful, I have pictured the one most commonly found in the western United States.

Some edible plants can be poisonous unless prepared with caution; others are easily confused with poisonous plants. To aid and caution readers, a † precedes each of these.

Amaranth
Amaranthus retroflexus
Food

Arrowhead
Sagittaria latifolia
Food

Arrowleaf Balsamroot
Balsamorrhiza sagittata
Food

Colorplate 1

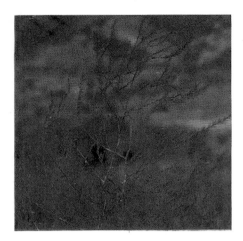

Asparagus
Asparagus officinalis
Food

Beeplant
Cleome lutea
Food

Beeplant
Cleome serrulata
Food

Colorplate 2

†Biscuit-root
Cymopterus bulbosus
Food, Medicine

Blazing Star
Mentzelia laevicaulis
Food

Bluegrass
Poa longiligula
Food

Colorplate 3

†Bracken Fern
Pteridium aquilinum
Food

†Bracken Fern
Pteridium aquilinum
Food

Bristlegrass
Setaria viridis
Food

Colorplate 4

Bulrush
Scirpus
Food, Fiber

Bulrush
Scirpus acutus
Food, Fiber

Burdock
Arctium minus
Food, Medicine

Colorplate 5

Burdock
Arctium minus
Food, Medicine

Burreed
Sparganium euricarpum
Food

†Camas
Camassia quamash
Food

Colorplate 6

†Camas
Camassia quamash
Food

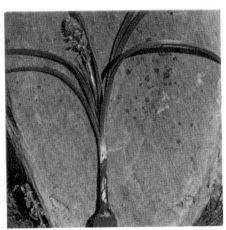

†Camas—Death Camas
Zigadenus paniculatus
Poisonous

Cattail
Typha latifolia
Food, Medicine, Tinder,
Fiber, Tools

Colorplate 7

†Chokecherry
Prunus virginiana
Food, Medicine, Tools

Cliffrose
Cowania mexicana
Tinder, Fiber

Cottonwood
Populus deltoides
Food, Tinder

Colorplate 8

Currant
Ribes
Food, Tools

Dogbane
Apocynum cannabinum
Tinder, Fiber

†Elderberry
Sambucus caerulea
Food

Evening Primrose
Oenothera hookeri
Food

Goldenrod
Solidago
Food

Greasewood
Sarcobatus
Food—Tools

Colorplate 10

Ground Cherry
Physalis fendleria
Food

Groundsel
Senecio
Food

Hairgrass
Deschampsia elongata
Food

Colorplate 11

Heron's Bill
Erodium cicutarium
Food

Heron's Bill
Erodium cicutarium
Food

Horsetail
Equisetum hyemale
Food

Colorplate 12

Indian Potato
Orogenia linariifolia
Food

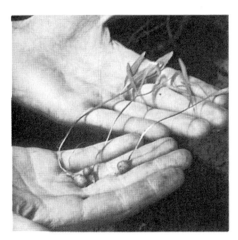

Indian Potato
Orgenia linariifolia
Food

Indian Ricegrass
Oryzopsis hymenoides
Food

Colorplate 13

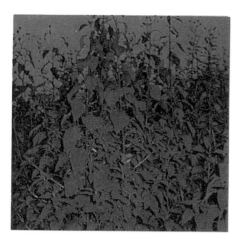

Jerusalem Artichoke
Helianthus tuberosus
Food

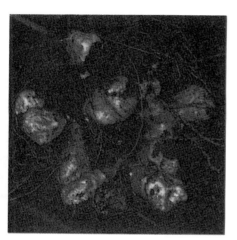

Jerusalem Artichoke
Helianthus tuberosus
Food

Juniper
Juniperus osteosperma
Food

Colorplate 14

Juniper
Juniperus osteosperma
Food, Tinder, Fiber

Lamb's Quarter
Chenopodium album
Food

Mallow
Malva neglecta
Food

Colorplate 15

Maple
Acer negundo
Food

†Milkweed
Asclepias speciosa
Food, Fiber

Miner's Lettuce
Montia perfoliata
Food

Colorplate 16

Mint
Mentha
Food

Mint
Mentha
Food

Mint
Nepeta cataria
Food

Colorplate 17

Mormon Tea
Ephedra
Food

Mountain Dandelion
Agoseris aurantiaca
Food

Mule's Ears
Wyethia amplexicaulis
Food

Colorplate 18

Mullein
Verbascum thapsus
Medicine, Tinder

Mustard
Brassica nigra
Food

Mustard
Cardaria draba
Food

Mustard
Lepidium perfoliatum
Food

Nettle
Urtica gracilis
Food, Medicine, Tinder, Fiber

†Oak
Quercus gambelii
Food

Colorplate 20

†Onion
Allium acuminatum
Food, Medicine

†Onion
Allium textile
Food, Medicine

Oregon Grape
Mahonia aquifolium
Food

Colorplate 21

Oregon Grape
Mahonia fremontii
Food

Piñon Pine
Pinus edulis
Food

Plantain
Plantago lanceolata
Food, Medicine

Colorplate 22

Prickly Lettuce
Lactuca scariola
Food

Prickly Lettuce
Lactuca scariola
Food

Prickly Pear Cactus
Opuntia phaeacantha
Food

Colorplate 23

Prickly Pear Cactus
Opuntia polyacantha
Food

Purslane
Portulaca oleracea
Food

†Rabbitbrush
Chrysothamnus nauseosus
Food

Colorplate 24

Raspberry
Rubus idaeus
Food

Red Clover
Trifolium pratense
Food

Reed
Phragmites communis
Food, Tinder, Fiber, Tools

Colorplate 25

Rose
Rosa
Food, Medicine, Tools

Sagebrush
Artemisia tridentata
Tinder, Fiber

Salsify
Tragopogon dubius
Food

Colorplate 26

Salsify
Tragopogon dubius (yellow)
Tragopogon porrifolius (purple)
Food

Samphire
Salicornia pacifica
Food

Sego Lily
Calochortus nuttallii
Food

Serviceberry
Amelanchier alnifolia
Food, Medicine, Tools

†Sorrel Dock
Rumex hymenosepalus
Food, Medicine

†Sour Dock
Rumex crispus
Food, Medicine

Colorplate 28

Spring Beauty
Claytonia lanceolata
Food

Strawberry
Fragaria vesca
Food

Sumac
Rhus trilobata
Food

Sunflower
Helianthus annuus
Food, Tinder

Thistle
Cirsium undulatum
Food, Tinder

Umbrella Plant
Eriogonum alpinum
Food

Colorplate 30

Violet
Erythronium grandiflorum
Food

Watercress
Rorippa nasturium-aquaticum
Food

Waterleaf
Hydrophyllum capitatum
Food

Colorplate 31

†Wild Hyacinth
Brodiaea douglasii
Food

Yarrow
Achillea millefolium
Medicine

Yellow Fritillary
Fritillaria pudica
Food

Colorplate 32

Index

Picture Credits

Black and White

Pictures by Dan Smith, Jr., Evard Gibby, Ural Latham, Stan Macbean, Pat Wright, Larry Dean Olsen, Paul Milberg, Doug Martin, Scott Pentzer, Pauline Sanchez, and William Whitiker.

Color

Pictures by Dan Smith, Nature Graphics, Provo, Utah, except for

Beeplant; *Cleome lutea* (colorplate 2): Bill Ratcliffe

Biscuit-root (colorplate 3): Stanley L. Welsh

Blazing Star (colorplate 3): Walter P. Cottam

Bluegrass (colorplate 3):Stanley L. Welsh

Bracken Fern, seedhead (colorplate 4): Walter P. Cottam

Burreed (colorplate 6): Vard Jones

Camas (colorplates 6, 7): Walter P. Cottam

Chokecherry (colorplate 8): Vard Jones

Cliffrose (colorplate 8): Bill Ratcliffe

Elderberry; *Sambucus caerulea* (colorplate 9): Vard Jones

Greasewood; *Sarcobatus* (colorplate 10): Evard Gibby

Indian Potato (colorplate 13): Stanley L. Welsh

Indian Potato, bulbs (colorplate 13):Stan Macbean

Miner's Lettuce (colorplate 16): Vard Jones

ntain Dandelion (colorplate 18): Vard Jones

Ears (colorplate 18):Walter P. Cottam

colorplate 27): Vard Jones

colorplate 28): Vard Jones

rplate 28): Walter P. Cottam

plate 29): Vard Jones

Stan Macbean

32): Walter P. Cottam

32): Walter P. Cottam